THE SEPARATION OF GOVERNMENTAL POWERS

IN HISTORY, IN THEORY, AND IN THE CONSTITUTIONS

BY
WILLIAM BONDY, L.L.B., Ph.D.
Sometime Seligman Fellow in Political Science

THE LAWBOOK EXCHANGE, LTD.
UNION, NEW JERSEY

1998

ISBN 1-886363-65-X

Printed in the United States of America
On Acid-Free Paper

Please see catalogue at rear of this book
for other titles reprinted by:

The Lawbook Exchange, Ltd.
965 Jefferson Avenue
Union, New Jersey 07083-8605

http://www.lawbookexc.com

Library of Congress Cataloging-in-Publication Data

Bondy, William, d. 1871.
Separation of governmental powers in history, in theory, and in the constitutions / by William Bondy.
p. cm.
Originally published: New York : Columbia College, 1896. (Studies in history, economics and public law ; v. 5, no. 2)
Includes bibliographical references.
ISBN 1-886363-65-X (cloth : acid-free paper)
1. Separation of powers—United States. I. Title. II. Series:
JK305.B7. 1998
320.473'04—dc21

98-44994
CIP

STUDIES IN HISTORY, ECONOMICS AND PUBLIC LAW

EDITED BY
THE UNIVERSITY FACULTY OF POLITICAL SCIENCE
OF COLUMBIA COLLEGE.

Volume V] [Number 2

THE SEPARATION OF GOVERNMENTAL POWERS

IN HISTORY, IN THEORY, AND IN THE CONSTITUTIONS

BY

WILLIAM BONDY, LL.B., Ph.D.

Sometime Seligman Fellow in Political Science

COLUMBIA COLLEGE
NEW YORK
1896

TABLE OF CONTENTS

CHAPTER X

CHAPTER XI

CHAPTER XII

CHAPTER XIII

CHAPTER XIV

CHAPTER XV

PART IV

The Legislature and the Executive

CHAPTER XVI

CHAPTER XVII

CHAPTER XVIII

PART V

The Executive and the Courts

CHAPTER XIX

CHAPTER XX

PART VI

Quasi Powers

CHAPTER XXI

CHAPTER XXII

PART I

THE SEPARATION OF GOVERNMENTAL POWERS IN HISTORY, IN THEORY, AND IN THE CONSTITUTIONS

CHAPTER I

THE HISTORICAL DEVELOPMENT OF THE SEPARATION OF GOVERNMENTAL POWERS

In every state, be it monarchic, aristocratic or democratic, there is a tendency to distribute the principal powers of government among distinct governmental organizations.[1]

The earliest dawn of civilization discloses, as the most primitive form of political organization, a warfaring society grouped about a victorious chief. This powerful personage is supposed to represent the fittest product of the period of barbaric liberty and self-help, which immediately preceded the period of governmental organization. The chieftain's superiority in valor convinces his superstitious admirers, as well as himself, that he is of divine descent.[2] This superstition invests him with a halo of glory and clothes him with sovereign power. The religious sanction secures reverence for his per-

[1] For the sense in which the term "State" is used herein, see "The Idea and Conception of the State" and "The Forms of the State," Burgess' *Pol. Sc. and Const. Law*, book ii, chapts. 1 and 3. See, also, "Tests of Governmental Forms," Burgess' *Pol. Sc. and Const. Law*, vol. 2, pt. ii, bk. 3, pp. 1, 8.

[2] "The common god of the English people, as of the whole German race, was Woden, the war god, whom every German tribe held to be the first *ancestor* of its kings."—Green, *A Short History of the English People*, p. 42. See also "The Origin of the State," Burgess' *Pol. Sc. and Const. Law*, bk. ii, ch. 2.

son and obedience for his laws. He experiences no opposition in immediately exercising all governmental powers. He is priest, war chief, judge and legislator.[1]

As war begets the king, so peace begets the judge and legislator. As his followers become peaceable and civilized, the king is appealed to for the enforcement of internal order and justice rather than for protection against external force. As these appeals grow numerous and the duty of satisfying them becomes more intricate, the sovereign, either as a matter of convenience, or in order to secure greater sanction for his acts and decisions, calls about him a council of wise and powerful men to hear, and to assist in determining, the questions presented, and also to advise him in the administration of his government.

This royal council, owing to the fact that the functions required in determining individual appeals differ from those required in formulating rules to be observed in the administration of government, soon develops into two distinct bodies, the legislature and the judicial court.

Notwithstanding the existence of these two advisory bodies, the king continues to execute his own will, which is still the supreme law. But, the intimacy necessarily arising between the king and his advisers soon breeds contempt. The shortcomings of the sovereign disclose to the wise and powerful men whom he has invited to assist him, the pious fraud which he has been exercising upon them. As they assert themselves, the sovereignty passes from the king to the lords; the state passes from the monarchic to the aristocratic form. The nobles, possessed of the sovereign power of the state, can now themselves assume, or can delegate to such authorities as they deem proper, the powers which the government may be called upon to exercise. They generally satisfy themselves by exercising or participating in the exercise of an unlimited

[1] See Maine, *Early Law and Custom*, ch. vi, p. 160.

legislative authority. Self-interest, if not convenience, prevents them from asserting with impunity all governmental authority. They dare not abolish the courts or the kingship, lest by so doing they may reveal to the masses their own discovery of the humble origin of their king. They fear lest in the absence of a general belief in the divine source of authority, the people may he led to consider their own right to assume sovereign powers. The barons therefore of their own accord now employ the king as their agent to execute their laws, and they likewise employ the courts to construe them.

When at last enlightenment and education have sufficiently spread state-consciousness among the masses, and the sovereign power in fact has passed from the nobility to the people, the latter resent the power of the few to concentrate or distribute at their pleasure all governmental authority. They know that where executive, legislative and judicial power may be assumed by a single person, or body of persons, there can be no guarantee against the exertion of dreaded despotic power. Hence, in delegating and distributing governmental power, and in creating and organizing governmental agencies, they endeavor to secure themselves as far as possible against the exercise of despotic power by the government which they establish, or by any part thereof.

Whereas, in a monarchic form of state, the sovereign power is generally identified in some manner with the executive department of its government, and, in the aristocratic form of state, in some manner with the legislative department of its government, the conditions materially change when the state has become democratic, that is, when the sovereign power has passed from the nobility to the masses. Owing to the great numbers of which the democratic state is composed, it is impracticable in fact, if possible in theory, for such state to exercise governmental authority immediately, or even to be identified in any manner whatsoever with any of the departments exercising governmental powers. The democratic state accordingly delegates the powers of government to organizations distinct from its own original sovereign organization. It generally delegates the principal powers of government to the already naturally and historically developed departments, the executive, legislative and judicial departments; and it organizes and employs each of these departments as its agent. But, since neither of these departments any longer exercises sovereign powers, but only delegated authority, and since each owes its existence to the will of the state only, and not to the will of any of the other departments, each is now independent of and co-ordinate with the others.

This tendency of a state, be it monarchic, aristocratic or democratic, to distribute its principal powers of government among distinct organizations, may briefly be illustrated by the history of England, which country first attracted the attention of the philosopher to the relation existing between the separation of governmental powers, and well-regulated civil liberty.

Shortly after the settlement of the Anglo-Saxons in England, their king summoned about him the witenagemote, or assembly of wise men, whom he consulted about the government of his state. Subsequently the witenagemote not only made laws, imposed taxes, concluded treaties, and advised the king as to the appointment and removal of officers, but it also exercised jurisdiction as a supreme court. Incessant wars, however, checked the further development of the witenagemote.[1]

After the Norman conquest we again find all public functions concentrated in the king. He was the state as well as the government. In the exercise of his governmental powers, the king was soon assisted by a council known as the Curia Regis. After a time, a portion of this body, at first specially charged with the management of judicial and revenue business, developed into a court; the council, by addition to it of representatives from the cities and boroughs, becoming the Parliament.

[1] Green, *A Short History of the English People*, pp. 66, 607, 685.

When, in about the year 1215, the sovereign power over England had passed from the kingship to the nobility, the barons, the state itself, assumed the power of making laws, which were even to govern the king himself. But they did not abolish the kingship. They reduced it from the position of sovereign to that of the executive department of their government.

When, by the year 1832, the sovereign power had finally passed from the nobility to the masses of England, the state adopted as its governmental agencies the kingship, the judiciary, and the parliament.[1]

[1] See "Formation of the Const. of Gt. Britain," Burgess' *Pol. Sc. and Const. Law*, bk. iii, ch. i.

The whereabouts of the legislative, judicial and executive powers in ancient and modern states, and the history of the theory of the separation of powers, are learnedly considered by Fuzier-Herman in a book entitled *La Separation des Pouvoirs*.

CHAPTER II

THE THEORY OF THE SEPARATION OF GOVERNMENTAL POWERS

THE analysis of government into three parts is as old as Aristotle. He already indicated the distinction existing between the three departments. In his Politics, he says that in every state there are three divisions: the general assembly deliberating upon public affairs (τὸ Βουλευόμενον περὶ τῶν κοινῶν), a body of magistrates (τὸ περί τὰς αρχάς), and a judiciary (τὸ δικάζον).[1]

Cicero asserted "Statu esse optimo constitutam rem publicam, quæ ex tribus generibus illis, regali et optumati et populari, confusa modice."[2]

Milton, in his "Ready and Easy Way to establish a Free Commonwealth," advocated the concentration of all powers in one body. According to Turgot's idea of a perfect government, a single assembly is to be possessed of all authority, legislative, executive and judicial.[3]

The tripartite division of the powers of government escaped further serious notice until John Locke in his treatise on Civil Government declared that in every state there were three powers, the legislative, executive and federative.

[1] John Adams says that the practicability of a republic in which there is a governor, a senate, and house of representatives, has been doubted by Tacitus, though he admitted the theory to be laudable. (Adams' *Defense of the American Constitutions*, preface, page 19.) Tacitus said "Cunctas nationes et urbes populus aut primores aut singuli regunt: delecta ex iis et consociata rei publicae forma laudari facilius quam evenire, vel si evenit, haud diuturna esse potest." (Tacitus, *Ann.*, lib. iv. cap. xxxiii.)

[2] Cicero's *De Re Publica*, Lib. II (*Fragmenta*).

[3] See Adams' *Def. of the American Const.*, pp. 365, *et seq.;* Story's *Commentaries on the Const.*, sec. 520, n. 3; *La Sep. des Pouvoirs*, pp. 8, 10, 54.

Speaking of federative power, he says, "This therefore contains the power of war and peace, leagues and alliances, and all transactions with all persons and communities without the commonwealth, and may be called federative, if any one pleases."

It therefore appears that by federative power Locke meant what is now commonly known as diplomatic power.[1]

He advocated placing federative and executive power in the hands of the same person.[2]

He maintained that "the legislative and executive powers are in distinct hands in all moderated monarchies and well-framed governments." But it is surprising that he overlooked the importance of the independence of judicial power in every government, since he understood justice to be the end of government.

His classification of powers as legislative, executive, and federative, is unscientific, especially if he meant to base it on the *nature* of such powers, because the proper exercise of diplomatic power generally requires the exercise of powers legislative, executive and even judicial in their nature.

His recognition of only the executive and legislative powers of a government, and his rejection of the judicial power, has been affirmed by publicists who maintain that the judicial is only a subdivision of the executive power.[3]

Montesquieu was the first to demonstrate that the separation of governmental powers is indispensable to civil liberty. He was the first to introduce the theory of the separation of governmental powers as a fundamental principle of our modern political science.

"When the legislative and executive powers are united in the same person or body," says Montesquieu, "there can be

[1] See post, page 76.

[2] Locke on *Civil Government*, chap. xii; *La Separation des Pouvoirs*, pp. 11 164, 178, 280.

[3] *La Separation des Pouvoirs*, pp. 11, 165.

no liberty, because apprehensions might arise lest the *same* monarch or senate should *enact* tyrannical laws, to execute them in a tyrannical manner." Again, "There is no liberty, if the judicial power be not separated from the legislative and executive. Were it joined with the legislative, the life and liberty of the subject would be exposed to arbitrary control, for the *judge* would then be the legislator. Were it joined to the executive power, the judge might behave with the violence of an oppressor. There would be an end of everything, were the same man or the same body, whether of nobles or of the people, to exercise these three powers, that of enacting laws, that of executing the public resolutions, and that of trying the causes of individuals."[1]

Blackstone reaches the same conclusion. He says: "Whereever the right of making and enforcing the law is vested in the same man or one and the same body of men, there can be no public liberty. The magistrate may enact tyrannical laws and execute them in a tyrannical manner, since he is possessed, in his quality of dispenser of justice, with all the power which he as legislator thinks proper to give himself."[2] As to the necessity of the separation of the judicial from the legislative and executive power, he says, "Were it joined with the legislative, the life, liberty, and property of the subject would be in the hands of arbitrary judges whose decisions would be regulated only by their opinions, and not by any fundamental principles of law; which though legislators may depart from, yet judges are bound to observe. Were it joined with the executive, this union might soon be an overbalance of the legislative."[3]

Many minor advantages which are gained by a division of governmental powers readily suggest themselves. Thus, where the legislative and judicial powers are exercised by distinct

[1] *Esprit des Lois*, livre xi, chapitre vi, "De la Constitution d' Angleterre."

[2] *Commentaries*, vol. i, p. 146.

[3] *Commentaries*, 269.

bodies, the general laws are made by one body of men without foreseeing whom they may affect, and when made, they must be applied by the other, let them affect whom they will. The legislature will then have no private interests to serve, consequently its laws will be suggested by considerations of universal effects and tendencies, which always produce impartial and commonly advantageous laws.[1]

Only one criticism upon Montesquieu's theory seems to merit consideration. It has been said that the judicial is not distinguishable from the executive power, properly speaking, but is only a subdivision of the latter. All that is required, so it is argued, to carry on government, is that the law should be *expressed* and *executed.* Accordingly, two powers appear originally in every state, the legislative and the executive; and of these the latter, the executive power, is generally divided into two organs: (1) the administrative, which is active; and (2) the judicial, which is inactive, has no initiative, and is only exercised when a controversy arises.[2]

It seems, however, that judicial power is executive only in the sense in which legislative power is executive. Every department of government and every governmental power is executive in so far as it executes the will of the state. Every department of government is organized, and every power of government is exercised, for the express purpose of *executing* that will. Neither department executes the independent will of any of the other departments, except so far as the will of the other departments is also the will of the state.

It might with equal propriety be said that all that is required to carry on government is that laws should be expressed and executed, and that two powers appear in every state, the legislative and the executive; that the legislative power is generally divided into two organs, the legislative, which is active, and which at its pleasure interprets and expresses the will of

[1] Paley's *Moral Philosophy*, book vi, chap. viii.

[2] *La Separation des Pouvoirs*, pp. 12, 179 n., 295.

the state, and the judicial, which is inactive and has no initiative, but which interprets and expresses the will of the state whenever a legal controversy arises as to what that will is.

Nor is it exact to say that two powers appear originally in every state, the legislative and the executive. The state from the first moment of its existence possesses every conceivable power.[1] What may be true is that historically the state established a distinct executive and legislative department of government before it established a distinct judicial department.[2]

Should it be conceded that the judicial is not theoretically distinguishable from the executive power, or even from the legislative power, this would not conflict with the theory of Montesquieu, which, without distinguishing between the nature of the different governmental powers, asserts that it is indispensable to civil liberty that the power of enacting laws, and of interpreting and executing them, be these powers alike or different in their nature, should be vested in three departments distinct and separate from each other.

[1] "L' état est fait sur le modèle de l' homme, il y a dans l' état comme une raison qui médite, comme une volonté qui agit, comme un sens moral qui ramène tous les cas particuliers aux règles générales tracées par la raison, par la conscience." *La Separation des Pouvoirs*, p. 18.

[2] Montesquieu says, "Il y a, dans chaque état, trois sortes de pouvoirs, la puissance législative, la puissance exécutrice des choses qui dépendent du droit des gens, et la puissance exécutrice de celles qui dépendent du droit civil. . . . On appellera cette dernière la puissance de juger; et l' autre, simplement la puissance exécutrice de l' état." *Esprit des Lois*, Liv. xi, c. vi. For criticisms of Montesquieu's theory see *La Separation des Pouvoirs*, p. 181 *et seq.*

CHAPTER III

THE DISTRIBUTING CLAUSES IN THE CONSTITUTION OF THE UNITED STATES AND IN THE COMMONWEALTH CONSTITUTIONS

It now becomes proper to refer to the unanimity with which the theory of the separation of governmental powers was accepted by the American Revolutionists. In his farewell address Washington says: "The spirit of encroachment tends to consolidate the powers of all departments in one, and thus to create, whatever the form of government, a real despotism." James Madison forcibly says: "The accumulation of all powers, legislative, executive, and judicial, in the same hands, whether of one, a few, or many, whether hereditary, self-appointed, or elective, may justly be pronounced the very definition of tyranny."[1] In this maxim Thomas Jefferson thoroughly concurred. He says: "The concentrating these in the same hands is precisely the definition of despotic government. It will be no alleviation that these powers will be exercised by a plurality of hands, and not by a single one. One hundred and seventy-three despots would surely be as oppressive as one."[2] John Adams thought: "It is by balancing each of these three powers against the other two, that the efforts in human nature toward tyranny can alone be checked and restrained and any degree of freedom preserved."[3]

"I agree," says Hamilton, "that there is no liberty if the power of judging be not separated from the legislative and executive powers."[4]

In more modern times, Webster says: "The separation of

[1] *Federalist*, no. xlvii.

[2] *Notes on Virginia*, p. 195.

[3] *Works of John Adams*, p. 186.

[4] *Federalist*, no. xlviii.

the departments so far as practicable, and the preservation of clear lines between them, is the fundamental idea in the creation of all our constitutions, and doubtless the continuance of regulated liberty depends on maintaining these boundaries."[1]

Justice Miller says: "It is believed to be one of the chief merits of the American system of written constitutional law that all powers entrusted to the government, whether state or national, are divided into the three grand departments, the executive, the legislative and the judicial; that the functions appropriate to each of these branches of government shall be vested in a separate body of public servants, and that the perfection of the system requires that the lines which separate and divide these departments shall be broadly and clearly defined. It is also essential to the successful working of the system, that the persons entrusted with power in any one of these branches shall not be permitted to encroach upon the powers confided to the others, but that each shall by the law of its creation be limited to the exercise of the powers appropriate to its own department, and no others."[2]

Great Britain governed each of the thirteen American commonwealths through a governor, legislature, and courts, with such powers and jurisdiction in each of these departments as its parliament willed.

When the united colonists relieved themselves of their subjection to what had become a foreign sovereignty, and they themselves assumed sovereign powers, they preserved these three departments in each one of their commonwealths, as their chief local governmental organs therein.

When they adopted the Articles of Confederation, they established a very limited central government, but retained for their local governments the three departments already existing in each of their commonwealths. The whole power of the central government they vested in a Congress, consisting of a

[1] *Webster's Works*, vol. iv, p. 122.

[2] Kilbourn *vs.* Thompson, 103 U. S. 188.

single body. "The organization of the whole powers of the general government in a single assembly without any separate or distinct distribution of the executive, judicial and legislative functions," Judge Story considered one of the serious defects of the Confederation, which ultimately led to its decline and fall.[1]

Of the twelve commonwealths which, prior to 1787, had adopted constitutions, six had inserted in their organic law a general distributing clause, expressly distributing the principal governmental powers among the legislative, executive, and judicial departments of their governments. These were Georgia, Maryland, Massachusetts, New Hampshire, North Carolina, and Virginia. The first constitution of Massachusetts, adopted in 1780, already provided that "in the government of this commonwealth, the legislative department shall never exercise the executive and judicial powers or either of them; the executive shall never exercise the legislative and judicial powers or either of them; the judiciary shall never exercise legislative or executive powers or either of them: to the end that it may be a government of laws and not of men."[2] The constitution of New Hampshire adopted in 1784 declared that "the legislative, executive, and judiciary powers ought to be kept as separate from and independent of each other as the nature of a free government will admit, or as is consistent with that chain of connection that binds the whole fabric of the constitution in one indissoluble bond of unity and amity."[3] Maryland adopted the maxim in the most unqualified terms, declaring "that the legislative, executive and judicial powers of government ought to be forever separate and distinct from each other."[4]

[1] *Commentaries on the Const.*, p. 189. See *Federalist*, no. xxii, where Hamilton says that the want of a judiciary power crowned the defects of the Confederation.

[2] See Poore's *Federal and State Constitutions; Federalist*, no. xlvii.

[3] Art. 37, Poore's *Federal and State Constitutions*, p. 1280.

[4] Art. 6, "Constitution adopted 1777," Poore's *Federal and State Constitutions*, p. 817. See also *Constitution of Virginia of 1776*, *Constitution of Georgia of 1777*, art. 1, and *Constitution of North Carolina of 1776*, art. 4. Virginia was the first State which introduced the clause into her organic law.

The authorities above referred to suffice to show how saturated with the philosophy of Montesquieu were the minds of those distinguished statesmen who, having conquered for us our independence, firmly secured our liberty. It is, therefore, not surprising for us to find that when the American state, as represented in the National Convention of 1787, was about to dispense governmental powers, it adopted as its first resolution that "a national government ought to be established, consisting of a supreme legislature, judiciary, and executive."[1] "From this fundamental proposition sprang the subsequent organization of the whole government of the United States, and it lies at the bottom of all our institutions, state as well as national."[2]

Since that time all the commonwealths, excepting New York, Pennsylvania, Ohio, Wisconsin, Kansas, Delaware, North Dakota, and Washington, have enacted a general distributing clause expressly providing for the tripartite division of governmental powers among the legislative, executive, and judicial departments. For instance, the present constitution of Connecticut provides that the powers of government shall be divided into three distinct departments, and each of them confided to a separate magistracy, to wit: those which are legislative to one, those which are executive to another, and those which are judicial to another. Of those that have adopted the clause, all excepting Rhode Island, Connecticut, and North Carolina have further provided that no person or collection of persons exercising the functions of one department shall assume or discharge the functions of any other; and all excepting Rhode

[1] *Journals of the Convention*, pp. 82, 83, 129, 207, 215. Specific provisions separating governmental powers were inserted into the constitution of 1791 of Po land, the constitutions of 1791 and 1795 of France, and the Hawaiian constitution of 1894. In the conference of 1887, between England, Germany, and the United States in regard to Samoa, Mr. Bayard, then Secretary of State of the United States, objected to the proposed German plan for the government of the islands on the ground that it ultimately vested legislative, judicial, and executive powers in the same person.

[2] Story's *Com. on the Const.*, sec. 519.

Island, Connecticut, New Jersey, North Carolina, Louisiana, New Hampshire, Massachusetts, Maryland, Virginia, West Virginia, and South Carolina, further qualify the provision by adding that the powers should be separated *except* in cases expressly directed or permitted by their constitutions.[1]

The constitution of South Dakota prescribes: "The powers of the government of the state are divided into three distinct departments—the legislative, executive, and judicial; and the powers and duties of each are prescribed by this constitution."[2]

Although the Constitution of the United States and the constitutions of New York, Pennsylvania, Ohio, Wisconsin, Kansas, Delaware, Washington, and North Dakota contain no general distributing clause, yet the constitution of Ohio provides that the legislature can exercise no judicial powers not expressly conferred by the constitution; and the constitution of every commonwealth, excepting New York, expressly vests by three separate provisions the *legislative power in the legislature, the executive in the governor, and the judicial in the judiciary.*

As a result of the first resolution adopted by the Constitutional Convention of 1787, the Constitution of the United States also provides that "all legislative powers herein granted shall be vested in a Congress of the United States which shall consist of a Senate and House of Representatives;"[3] that "the executive power shall be vested in a President of the United States of America;"[4] and that "the judicial power of the United States shall be vested in one Supreme Court and in such inferior courts as Congress may from time to time ordain and establish."[5] But the Constitution of the United States does not prohibit commonwealth legislatures from exercising judicial functions.[6]

[1] Stimson's *American Statute Law*, sec. 200.

[2] Art. ii.

[3] *Constitution of the United States*, art. 1, Sec. 1.

[4] Art. 2, sec. 1.

[5] Art. 3, sec. 1.

[6] Satterlee *vs.* Mathewson, 2 Peters, 413. There is no provision in the Consti-

By applying well-known rules of construction to their constitutions, all commonwealths, including New York, have distributed their principal governmental powers among three independent departments, irrespective of the fact whether they have enacted a distributing clause or not. Since different classes of power in every commonwealth are apportioned to the different departments, and since all departments derive their authority from the same instrument, there is an implied exclusion of each department from exercising the functions conferred upon the others. The apportionment to the legislature of all legislative power does not sanction the exercise of executive or judicial power; and the granting of judicial power must be regarded as an exclusive grant covering the whole power, subject only to the limitations of the constitution itself.[1] On this subject, Judge Comstock said: "I entertain no doubt that, aside from the special limitations of the constitution, the legislature cannot exercise powers which are in their nature essentially judicial or executive. These are by the constitution distributed to other departments of the government. It is only the legislative power which is vested in the senate and assembly; but where the constitution is silent and there is no clear usurpation of the powers distributed to the other departments, I think there would be great difficulty and great danger in the attempt to define the limits of this power."[2] On still another occasion, the court, after referring to the distribution of powers in the Constitution of the United States, said:

tution of the United States prohibiting a commonwealth legislature from granting new trials and appeals.—Calder *vs.* Bull, 3 Dall. 386. "Before the United States Constitution was adopted every commonwealth, except as prohibited by its own constitution, might have passed a bill of attainder or *ex post facto* law as a general result of its sovereign legislative power, and such a prohibition would not be implied from a constitutional provision that the legislative, executive, and judicial departments shall be separate and distinct."—Story's *Com. on the Const.*, Sec. 1373. See Cooper *vs.* Telfaire, 4 Dall. 14.

[1] People *vs.* Draper, 15 N. Y. 532, 543.

[2] Wynehamer *vs.* People, 13 N. Y. 378, 391.

"Although no similar declaration is contained in the constitution of this state, still it is a recognized principle that in the division of powers among the great departments of government, the judicial power has been committed to the judiciary, the executive power has been committed to the executive department, and the legislative to the legislature, and that body has no power to assume the functions of the judiciary to determine controversies among citizens, or even to expound its own laws so as to control decisions of the court in respect to past transactions."[1] Chancellor Kent says: "If the provision that the legislative and judicial powers shall be preserved separate and distinct be not found in our own constitution, it exists there in substance in the organization and distribution of the powers of the departments, and in the declaration that the 'supreme legislative power' shall be vested in the Senate and the Assembly. No maxim has been more universally received and cherished as a vested principle of freedom; and without having recourse to the authority of elementary writers or to the popular conventions of Europe, we have a more commanding authority in the sense of the American people that the right to interpret the law does and ought to belong exclusively to the courts of justice."[2] The executive can do no legislative act, nor the legislature any executive act, and neither can exercise judicial authority.[3]

The case of the Supervisors of Elections[4] is the only one found in which a distinction is intimated on account of the distributing clause. The court in this case was called upon to decide upon the constitutionality of a law empowering the courts to designate supervisors of election. The court observed: "The statute in question acquires no support from the

[1] People ex rel. McDonald *vs.* Keeler, 99 N. Y. 463.

[2] Dash *vs.* Van Kleeck, 7 Johns. 477; Ogden *vs.* Blackledge, 2 Cranch, 272; People *vs.* Board of Supervisors, 16 N. Y. 432.

[3] Still *vs.* Corning, 15 N. Y. 297.

[4] 114 Mass. 247.

act of Congress conferring power to appoint similar officers upon the judges of the Circuit Court of the United States, or in the action of the judges pursuant thereto, because the Constitution of the United States does not *so explicitly* restrain the judges from exercising executive or political functions as does the constitution of this commonwealth, and so far as we are informed, without any question of constitutional power being raised or argued."[1] The court, however, admitted its power to appoint officers whom it designated as ministerial, and officers exercising powers judicial in their nature.

In addition to the distributing clause, there are also provisions in all the constitutions establishing the principal departments of government in such manner that each exists independently of the others, as well as provisions granting to each such powers as were deemed necessary in order to guard each against any undue control or interference by the others. Some of these provisions will be recognized as re-enactments of principles established in England by Parliament in order to insure its independence, and that of the courts against encroachments by the crown. Many of these, had they not been expressly constituted a part of our fundamental law, would have been made such by judicial construction, for without them the departments would not be independent.

To preserve their independence it is essential that no one department shall be dependent upon the others in tenure. The governors, the members of the legislature and the judges are accordingly, as a general rule, elected by the people of their respective commonwealths. The only exception to the uniformity of this rule is found in the case of the judges. They are in twenty-five commonwealths elected by the people. But in order to prevent political contamination from polluting the sources of justice, Rhode Island, Vermont, Virginia, South Carolina and Georgia provide for their election by the legisla-

[1] As to the constitutionality of the act of Congress, see *In re* Citizens of Cincinnati, 2 Flippin, 228.

ture, and the Constitutions of the United States, Massachusetts, Connecticut, New Hampshire, Delaware, Maine, Mississippi, Louisiana, New Jersey and Florida provide for their appointment by the chief executive officer, and, in some cases, for the confirmation of the appointment by a council or a branch of the legislature.[1]

To further insure the independence of the judiciary, some constitutions declare that the judges shall hold their offices during good behavior.[2]

Among the provisions securing a separation of the departments is that found in the Constitution of the United States, and the constitution of every commonwealth, that each house of the legislature shall be judge of the qualifications, elections and returns of its own members.[3]

The correctness of the decision of either house of the legislature that persons claiming seats therein have been duly elected members, cannot be questioned or inquired into by the executive or judicial departments;[4] and a law cannot be assailed as void because a portion of the members who voted for it, and without whose votes it would not have had the requisite majority, had been declared elected by the legislature in defiance of law, and to the exclusion of others who had a majority of legal votes.[5] Nor have the commonwealth courts jurisdiction

[1] Stimson's *American Statute Law*, art. 56; *Const. of North Dakota*, sec. 90; *of Wyoming*, art. 5, sec. 4; *of Washington*, art. 4, sec. 3; *of Montana*, art 8, sec. 6; *of South Dakota*, art. 5, sec. 1; *of Idaho*, art. 5, sec. 6; *Const. of United States*, art. 2, sec. 2, ¶ 2. For a comparative study of the organization and powers of each of the three main governmental departments in England, France, Germany, and the United States, see Burgess' *Pol. Sc. and Const. Law*, vol. 2. See *Federalist*, nos. 78–82.

[2] Stimson's *American Statute Law*, sec. 561; *United States Const.*, art. 3, sec. 1. See *Federalist*, no. 48, and Story's *Com. on the Constitution*, vol. 2, p. 416.

[3] Story's *Com. on the Constitution*, vol. 1, p. 604.

[4] Opinion of Judges, 56 N. H. 570. See State *vs.* Jarrett, 17 Md. 309; People *ex rel.* Sherwood *vs.* Bd. of Canvassers, 129 N. Y. 360.

[5] People *vs.* Mahany, 13 Mich. 481.

to decide whether the election of United States Senators by the commonwealth legislatures conforms to the regulations of Congress, or is void, such questions belonging exclusively to the United States Senate.[1]

The same necessity not existing therefor, the power to judge of the election of their own members is not possessed by municipal legislative bodies,[2] nor by boards of supervisors,[3] except when specially conferred by law.

In the absence of express constitutional prohibition, the legislature, having full power over legislative offices, may confer the power of deciding contested elections thereto upon the courts or any administrative board or officer, or assume the power itself.[4] The authority to try contested elections is not necessarily "judicial" within the constitutional requirement that the judicial power of the commonwealth shall be vested in the courts.[5] The legislature may make the decision of such administrative officer or board final and conclusive. Thus the decision of a school committee was held to be conclusive, which declared a seat in the school board vacant for want of legal election and qualification, because the person receiving the greatest number of votes was a woman.[6] In order to exclude the jurisdiction of the courts, the board's or officer's power finally to determine an election must be bestowed in unequivocal terms.[7] Otherwise the decision of the board or officer will be deemed concurrent and cumulative only. Such a decision will be regarded as temporarily binding upon the board, but will not prevent the courts from inquiring

[1] In re Executive Communications, 12 Fla. 686.

[2] People *vs.* Hall, 80 N. Y. 117.

[3] Robinson *vs.* Cheboygan Supervisors, 49 Mich. 321.

[4] State *vs.* Harmon, 31 Ohio St. 250.

[5] *Id.*

[6] Peabody *vs.* School Committee, 115 Mass. 383. See People *vs.* Fitzgerald, 41 Mich. 2; Doran *vs.* De Long, 48 Mich. 552.

[7] State *vs.* Kempf, 69 Wis. 470.

into the right to the office in behalf of the people of the commonwealth, upon proper application being made thereto.[1]

That jurisdiction to determine contested elections to the legislature shall be granted to the courts in every case has been strenuously advocated.[2]

In all commonwealths, except Kansas, it is prescribed that each house shall choose its own officers. Many constitutions, however, provide that the lieutenant-governor shall be president of the senate.[3]

Each house of the legislature is entrusted with the power to determine the rules of its own procedure, and to punish its members for disorderly behavior, and in some cases even to expel a member.[4]

Senators and representatives are generally by constitutional exemption privileged from arrest in all cases except treason, felony and breach of the peace, either during the session of the legislature or for some limited time before and after its session, or while members of the legislature.[5]

The constitutions of Kansas, Nebraska, Alabama, Arkansas, California, Missouri, Mississippi, Wisconsin, Indiana, Oregon and Colorado further provide that members of the legislature shall not be subject to *any process* during the session of the legis-

[1] People *vs.* Hall, 80 N. Y. 117.

[2] Burgess, *Pol. Sc. and Const. Law*, vol. 2, p. 114. See Bryce, *American Commonwealth*, 2d ed., p. 235.

[3] Stimson's *American Statute Law*, sec. 270. See Story, *Com. on Const.*, vol. 1, p. 540, for the reason for this exception.

[4] Stimson's *American Statute Law*, art. 27; *Const. of North Dakota*, secs. 48 and 49; *South Dakota*, art. 3, sec. 9; *Wyoming*, art. 3, sec. 12; *Washington*, art. 2, secs. 8, 9; *Montana*, art. 5, sec. 11; *Idaho*, art. 3, secs. 9, 11; *United States Const.*, art. 1, secs. 2, 3, 5. See Story, *Commentaries on Const.*, vol. 1, p. 657.

[5] Stimson's *American Statute Law*, sec. 273; *Const. of North Dakota*, sec. 42; *South Dakota*, art. 3, sec. 11; *Wyoming*, art. 3, sec. 16; *Washington*, art. 2, sec. 16; *Montana*, art. 5, sec. 15; *Idaho*, art. 3, sec. 7. See Cooley, *Const. Limitations*, pp. 546, 547; Story, *Com. on Const.*, vol. 1, p. 627.

lature, and Michigan further provides for the same immunity for fifteen days next before the commencement, and next after the termination of each session.[1] Necessarily, this same immunity, even in the absence of any statutory or constitutional provision to that effect, extends to the chief executive officer of every commonwealth as well as of the central government. Such officer is privileged from the jurisdiction of every court, magistrate and body over his person. He cannot be arrested or restrained of his personal liberty by anybody for anything, not even for the commission of murder. He is responsible only to that body which is empowered by the constitution to remove him. Even in the course of his trial before such body he cannot be arrested or in any manner restrained, nor forced to appear in person before such tribunal, or to give testimony, nor be deprived of any of his powers as chief executive officer.[2]

Because a power over a man's subsistence is in most cases a control over his will, the Constitution of the United States, and the constitutions of Maine, Ohio, Illinois, Tennessee, Missouri, Texas, California, Nevada, Georgia, Louisiana, Rhode Island, New York, Indiana, Minnesota, Maryland, Virginia, North Carolina, Kentucky, Arkansas, South Carolina, Mississippi, Alabama, North Dakota, Washington, Idaho, Montana, and Wyoming provide that the compensation of judges shall not be diminished during their continuance in office.[3]

In 1802, however, Congress passed an act depriving certain judges of their offices and therefore incidentally of the title to their salary.[4]

[1] Cooley, *Const. Limitations*, p. 160.

[2] Burgess, *Pol. Sc. and Const. Law*, vol. 2, p. 245; Durand *vs.* Hollins, 4 Blatch. 451.

[3] Stimson's *American Statute Law*, sec. 564; *Const. of North Dakota*, sec. 9; *Wyoming*, art. 5, sec. 17; *Washington*, art. 4, sec. 13; *Montana*, art. 8, sec. 29; *Idaho*, art. 5, sec. 27; *United States Const.*, art. 3, sec. 1; Story's *Com. on the Const.*, vol. 2, p. 439; *Federalist*, no. 79.

[4] Story, *Com. on Const.*, vol. 2, p. 442.

A provision similar to the foregoing is also generally found regarding the compensation of the chief executive officer.[1]

The organic law of every commonwealth except South Carolina, North Carolina, Mississippi, Florida, Nevada, California, North Dakota, Texas, and Washington provides that no member of the legislature shall be questioned elsewhere for any speech or debate in either house.[2] This provision, however, is unnecessary, for the protection of the legislators would probably be equally complete without it.[3]

Most commonwealths further provide that no person holding office shall be a member of either house of the legislature during his continuance in office.[4]

The revised constitution of New York of 1894 provides, in addition to the foregoing, that "the judges of the Court of Appeals and the justices of the Supreme Court shall not hold any other office or public trust, and that all votes for any of them for any other than a judical office given by the Legislature or the people shall be void."[5]

Finally, the chief executive and the judicial officers are not liable to removal, except in certain specified cases, in a certain prescribed manner, as by impeachment, by a vote of the legisture, or by the governor upon proper address by the legislature.[6]

Besides providing for the independent organization and existence of the main departments, and giving to each the neces-

[1] *Const. North Dakota*, sec. 84; *South Dakota*, art. 4, sec. 2; *Wyoming*, art. 4, sec. 13; *Washington*, art. 4, sec. 25; *Montana*, art. 5, sec. 31; *Idaho*, art. 4, sec. 19; *Federalist*, no. 73; Story, vol. 2, p. 324.

[2] Stimson's *American Statute Law*, art. 27; *Const. of Washington*, art. 2, sec. 17; *Montana*, art. 5, sec. 15; *Idaho*, art. 3, sec. 7. See Story, *Com. on the Const.*, vol. 1, p. 630.

[3] Cushing, *Law and Practice of Legislative Assemblies*, sec. 602.

[4] *Const. of North Dakota*, secs. 37, 39; *South Dakota*, art. 3, sec. 3; *Wyoming*, art. 3, sec. 8; *Washington*, art. 2, sec. 13; *Montana*, art. 5, sec. 7; *United States Constitution*, art. 1, sec. 6; *New York Const.*, art. 3, sec. 7.

[5] *New York Const.*, art. 6, sec. 10.

[6] Stimson's *American Statute Law*, art. 26.

sary powers for self-preservation, the fundamental law in many cases prohibits the departments from exercising powers which on account of their organization they are not thought capable of properly exercising, or expressly grants the departments such powers as they on account of their peculiar organization are best able to exercise.

Thus, besides the restriction contained in the Constitution of the United States prohibiting Congress and the commonwealths[1] from passing bills of attainder, the constitution of every commonwealth, except Delaware, New Hampshire, New York, North Carolina, Rhode Island, Tennessee, Louisiana, Indiana, Mississippi, Illinois, Iowa, Oregon and Kansas, provides that the legislature shall pass no bills of attainder.[2]

The constitutions of Vermont, Maryland, West Virginia, North Carolina, Missouri, Texas, Georgia and Alabama forbid the suspension of the writ of habeas corpus in any case whatsoever. In Massachusetts it can only be suspended on the most urgent occasion, and for a limited time, not exceeding twelve months, and in New Hampshire not exceeding three months.

In the remaining constitutions it is provided that the privilege of the writ shall not be suspended unless when, in case of rebellion or invasion, public safety may require it.[3]

In Rhode Island, Michigan, Maryland, Tennessee, and Arkansas, it is expressly prescribed that the writ can only be suspended by the legislature.

[1] *United States Const.*, art. I, secs. 9 and 10.

[2] The constitutions of Alabama, Massachusetts, Vermont, Connecticut, Pennsylvania, Maryland, Kentucky, Missouri, and Colorado, provide that no person can be attainted of treason or felony by the legislature.—Stimson's *Am. Statute Law*, sec. 138. The term bills of attainder includes bills of pain and penalties.—Story, *Com. on Const.*, vol. 2, p. 217 n.; Cooley's *Const. Limitations*, p. 314; *Ex parte* Garland, 4 Wall. 333; Fletcher *vs.* Peck, 6 Cr. 8; Cummings *vs.* Missouri, 4 Wall. 217.

[3] *United States Const.*, art. I, sec. 9; Stimson's *Am. Statute Law*, sec. 127; Story, *Com. on Const.*, vol. 2, p. 214 n.

In like manner by the constitutions of most commonwealths, laws can only be suspended by the legislature, or, as in some cases, by authority derived from the legislature.[1]

Some constitutions prohibit the legislature from auditing or allowing any private claim or account against the state.[2]

To the rule that the constitutions provide for the independent organization and existence of each of the departments, an exception is sometimes found in the case of the judiciary. The Constitution of the United States[3] and the constitutions of some commonwealths confer upon the legislature the power from time to time to ordain and establish inferior courts. In New Hampshire there are no constitutional provisions erecting courts, but the whole subject is left to the discretion of the legislature.

In the commonwealths in which the constitutions confer the judicial power upon certain *specified* courts, this must be understood to embrace the whole judicial power, and the legislature cannot in such case pass a statute abolishing any such courts, or vest any portion of such power elsewhere;[4] and where a constitution fixes the jurisdiction of a particular court, it is not competent for the legislature either to enlarge or abridge its jurisdiction.[5] Thus where the constitutional jurisdiction is appellate only, the legislature cannot confer upon it original jurisdiction in any case.[6]

Although the legislature cannot confer upon the courts which it is permitted to create by statute, jurisdiction in exclusion of that which the constitution gives to the courts estab-

[1] Stimson's *Am. Statute Law*, sec. 392.

[2] *Const. of New York*, art. 3, sec. 19. See Cole *vs.* State, 102 N. Y. 48; comp. *Const. of New York*, art. 7, sec. 6.

[3] Art. 1, sec. 8, and art. 3, sec. 1.

[4] Chandler *vs.* Nash, 5 Mich. 409.

[5] Gilbon *vs.* Templeton, 62 Texas, 555; State *vs.* Jones, 22 Ark. 331.

[6] State *vs.* Jones, 22 Ark. 331; Ward *vs.* Thomas, 2 Cald. (Tenn.) 565; State *vs.* Bank, 5 Sneed (Tenn.) 573; Marbury *vs.* Madison, 1 Cr. 137.

lished by itself,[1] yet it may vest a part of the jurisdiction of the constitutional courts, or a concurrent jurisdiction, in those tribunals which it creates by statute.[2]

The power to distribute judicial power, except so far as it has been done by the constitution, resting with the legislature,[3] with the exception of the creation of the Supreme Court, the power of Congress to create courts and confer upon them as much or as little jurisdiction pertaining to the United States government as it thinks best, is almost unlimited.[4]

The Constitution of the United States grants to Congress power to determine the number of judgeships which the Supreme Court shall contain. It has been shown that at the end of any term concluded by death, resignation, or impeachment of any of the judges, the legislature may modify or abolish that particular judgeship for the future. In this manner it is possible for the legislature virtually to disestablish even the Supreme Court at the conclusion of the term of the judges who may be holding at the time the legislature may adopt this destructive policy.[5]

Some constitutions vest the legislature with power to regulate and even to restrict the appellate jurisdiction of the higher courts.[6] In the absence of such constitutional provision, it would be part of the legislative power to point out the modes in which the appellate jurisdiction of the court shall be exercised.[7]

[1] Montrose *vs.* State, 61 Miss. 429.

[2] Commonwealth *vs.* Green, 58 Pa. St. 226; Borse *vs.* Preston, 111 U. S. 252; Ames *vs.* Kansas, 111 U. S. 449; Sharp *vs.* Robertson, 5 Gratt. (Va.) 518.

[3] Commonwealth *vs.* Hipple, 69 Pa. St. 9; State *vs.* New Brunswick, 42 N. J. 51.

[4] U. S. *vs.* Union Pac. R. R. Co., 98 U. S. 569; Story, *Com. on Const.*, vol. 2, p. 500, and cases cited.

[5] Burgess, *Pol. Sc. and Const. Law*, vol. 2, p. 320; Story, *Com. on Const.*, vol. 2, p. 409.

[6] *United States Const.*, art. 3, sec. 2; *Const. of New York*, art. 6, sec. 1.

[7] Haight *vs.* Gay, 8 Cal. 297.

Speaking of such provisions, Prof. Burgess says: "This power of the legislature over the judiciary is a most serious one. It places the appellate power of the court very nearly at the mercy of the legislature. It seems an unnecessary surrender of the independence of the court to require that things which can be better accomplished by the rules of court, shall wait upon the pleasure or, possibly, caprice of the legislature." [1]

The judiciary article of the new constitution of the state of New York provides that appeals from inferior and local courts shall be heard in the supreme court in such manner and by such justice or justices as the appellate divisions in the respective departments shall direct, unless otherwise provided by the legislature.[2]

It is now generally admitted that it is not necessary for the legislature to act and to designate the mode and manner in which courts are to proceed in order to enable the courts to exercise their constitutional powers and duties; and that the courts will discharge their duty by a course conformable to the common law in the absence of legislation upon the subject.[3]

Thus under the article of the United States Constitution, which provides that the Supreme Court shall have appellate jurisdiction with such exceptions and under such regulations as Congress shall make, it is supposed that no action of Congress is necessary to vest appellate jurisdiction in the Supreme Court, but that the same attaches *proprio vigore*, subject to be withdrawn or modified by Congress.[4]

While the jurisdiction of the courts may under some constitutions be almost wholly under the control of the regulating power of the legislature, it may be noted that there are certain

[1] *Pol. Sc. and Const. Law*, vol. 2, p. 331.

[2] Art. 6, sec. 5.

[3] State *vs.* Gleason, 12 Fla. 190.

[4] See Story, *Com. on the Const.*, vol. 2, p. 555; Durousseau *vs.* United States, 6 Cr. 307, 313; United States *vs.* Moore, 3 Cr. 159, 170, 172; *ex parte* McCardle, 7 Wall. 506.

incidental powers which are supposed to attach to them when duly organized without any positive enactment of the legislature. Such are the powers of the courts over their own officers, and the power to protect them and their members from being disturbed in the exercise of their functions. Among the powers supposed to inhere in a court when once established is the power to punish for contempt of its authority, which it would possess even in the absence of legislation expressly granting or regulating it.[1]

In considering the extensive power of the legislature in some cases to establish courts and to distribute judicial power among them in accordance with the constitution, the limitation effected upon it by the distributing clause should not be overlooked. The judicial power must be vested in courts and judges, as prescribed by the constitution, and can never be assumed by the legislature or delegated to the officers whom the constitutions designate as members of the executive department. Any body and any person to whom the legislature does delegate such power becomes a court or a judge, subject to the provisions of the constitution regarding such tribunal and officer.

[1] See *Ex parte* Bollman, 4 Cr. 75, 94; *Ex parte* Kearney, 7 Wheat. 37, 44; Anderson *vs.* Dunn, 6 Wheat. 204.

CHAPTER IV

THE BALANCE OF POWERS IN THEORY

SHOULD anything further be inferred from the fundamental principle laid down by Montesquieu, than that the whole power of one of these departments should not be exercised by the same hands which possess the whole power of either of the other departments, the result would be grievous in theory as well as in practice.

Considering that England did not resort to an absolute separation of powers or of the departments, and that England was the example referred to by Montesquieu, it is evident that the French philosopher did not intend to advocate the entire disjunction of the powers or departments.

Under the British constitution, the executive magistrate formed an integral part of the legislative authority. He alone had the prerogative of making treaties with foreign sovereigns, which, when made, had under certain limitations the force of legislative acts. The king appointed all members of the judicial department. One branch of the legislative department formed a great constitutional council to the executive chief. It was also the sole court of impeachment, and invested with supreme appellate jurisdiction in all other cases.

"From these facts, by which Montesquieu was guided, it may clearly be inferred that in saying, 'There can be no liberty where the legislative and executive powers are united in the same person,' or 'if the power of judging be not separated from the legislative and executive powers,' he did not mean that these departments ought to have no *partial agency* in, or no *control* over, the acts of each other. His meaning, as his own words import, and still more conclusively as illustrated by the example in his eye, can amount to no more than this; that where the *whole* power of one department is exercised by the same hands which possess the *whole* power of another department, the fundamental principles of a free government are subverted."[1] Blackstone says: "The total disjunction of them would in the end produce the same effects by causing that union against which it seems to provide."[2] If each department of government, being equal, could thwart the operations of the other, government would soon be at a dead-lock, since each, acting in defence of its own powers, would never lend its aid to the others.[3] Furthermore, these departments, on account of the differences which exist in their organization and functions, are unequal in the power of self-preservation. The legislative power is everywhere extending the sphere of its activity and drawing all powers into its impetuous vortex.[4] The action of the judicial and executive departments is always more or less dependent upon that of the legislature. Besides, the people are little apt jealously to guard against the encroachments made by the legislature, which they regard as the most direct representative of their will; and the great number of the law-making body, in which lies its strength, diminishes its sense of responsibility in trespassing upon the domain of the other departments. On the other hand, the courts and the executive are apt to be unpopular with the people. In the enforcement of their duties, they directly affect the interests of individuals.

That which these considerations would prepare one to expect, actually came to pass in the early history of Pennsylvania and Virginia. The first constitution of Virginia declared that the three great departments ought not to be intermixed. Jefferson,

[1] James Madison, *Federalist*, no. xlvii. See also *La Separation des Pouvoirs*, p. 177.

[2] *Commentaries*, book i, p. 154.

[3] Mill on *Representative Government*, p. 82.

[4] Madison, *Federalist*, no. xlvii.

commenting upon this provision, says, "No barrier was provided between these several powers," and then points out how the legislature, as a result of this, had encroached upon the judiciary and the executive.[1] The experience of Pennsylvania was not happier. The council of censors which assembled therein in 1783 to inquire whether the constitution had been preserved inviolate in every part, reported that the constitution had been violated by the legislative usurpation of executive and judicial powers, and that the salaries of the judges had been frequently varied.[2]

Jefferson, in a proposed constitution for Virginia, appended by him to his Notes on Virginia, suggested as a remedy against the encroachment of one department upon another, that the people should be appealed to by the invaded department.

Madison has conclusively shown the futility of this plan. He says that, as every appeal to the people would carry an implication of some defect in the government, frequent appeals would in a great measure deprive the government of that veneration which time bestows on everything, and without which perhaps the wisest and freest governments would not possess the requisite stability. Furthermore, whereas the courts and executive are likely to be unpopular and the legislature popular with the people, the same influences that secured the members of the legislature their election to that body, would secure for them their election to the convention which would, as the representative of the sovereign power of the state, decide the appeal. The members of the convention would be called upon to decide against themselves as legislators.[3]

Having separated the three departments from each other, the more difficult task remains of securing each against encroachments by the other. The true solution of this difficulty, says

[1] *Notes on the State of Virginia*, p. 195.

[2] *Federalist*, no. xlviii.

[3] *Federalist*, no. xlix.

Madison, is to permit each department to participate in the functions exercised by the others, so as to check but not so as to control them. The defect must be supplied by so contriving the interior structure of government that its several constituent parts may, by their mutual relations, be the means of keeping each other in their proper places. The greatest security against a gradual concentration of the several powers in the same department consists in giving those who administer each department the necessary constitutional means or personal motives to resist the encroachments of the other. But each department should have a will of its own. There is no method for producing this result but a partial participation of each in the powers of the others, and the introducing in all branches a system of checks and balances on which the safety of free institutions is found essentially to depend.[1]

[1] *Federalist*, 47, 48, 50, 51. These numbers of the *Federalist* were written to defend the Constitution of the United States against the violent attacks made upon it at the time of its adoption, on the ground that, although it professed to be founded upon a tripartite separation of governmental powers, yet it was chargeable with a departure from the principle, and therefore dangerous to civil liberty.

CHAPTER V

THE BALANCE OF POWERS IN THE CONSTITUTIONS

A MOST cursory examination of the American constitutions will reveal the fact that, notwithstanding the emphatic, and in some instances the unqualified terms in which the maxim of the separation of governmental powers is laid down, there is not, and there never has been, a single constitution in which some of the chief powers of government were not made dependent for their proper exercise upon the action of more than one of the governmental departments, and in which powers, historically or theoretically considered executive, have not been exercised by the legislative and judicial departments; in which powers considered judicial have not been exercised by the legislative and executive departments; and in which powers considered legislative in their nature have not been exercised by the executive and judicial departments.[1]

The best illustration of what may be accomplished by the balancing of powers, is the fact that the executive power in our country holds its ground not only by reason of its separation from and independence of the legislature, but also by reason of its participation in legislation. By means of his veto power the president cannot control, but may with a limited effect check legislation. "It was vested in the president doubtless as a guard against hasty and inconsiderate legislation, and

[1] "The Declaration of Rights and the Constitution are not to be interpreted as enjoining a complete separation between the several departments. Practically it has never been so in any of the States in whose fundamental law the principle has been asserted." Mayor *vs*. State, 15 Md. 376. See *Federalist*, no. 47, for the manner in which the early American constitutions provided for the admixture of powers.

against any acts inadvertently passed which might seem to encroach on the just authority of the other branches of the government."[1] Considering the purpose for which the veto power was vested in the executive, it ought to be employed chiefly *to prevent encroachments* by the legislature upon the constitutional prerogatives of the executive and to prevent unwise legislative changes in the existing means and measures of the administration.[2]

With only four exceptions the commonwealth constitutions vest a limited veto power in the executive. The four exceptional constitutions are those of Delaware, North Carolina, Ohio and Rhode Island, which commonwealths probably feared encroachments by the executive upon the powers of the legislative department.[3] In Ohio the ancient prejudice against the executive department seems still to survive. A resolution providing for a submission to the people of an amendment to the constitution, vesting the governor with the veto power, was in 1894 defeated in the lower branch of the legislature by a vote of 47 to 25.

Since important exigencies requiring legislation may arise at a time when the legislature is not in session, the chief executive under all the constitutions is vested with the power of convening extra sessions of the legislature on extraordinary occasions.[4]

In all commonwealths except New Jersey, Maryland, Virginia, New York, North Carolina, Tennessee, Indiana, Louisiana, Alabama, Missouri, Michigan, Texas, Wisconsin, Washington, Montana, Minnesota, Oregon, West Virginia, North

[1] *Webster's Works*, vol. 1, p. 267.

[2] Burgess, *Pol. Sc. and Const. Law*, vol. 2, p. 255.

[3] Stimson's *American Statute Law*, sec. 305; *Const. of North Dakota*, sec. 79; *South Dakota*, art. 4, sec. 9; *Wyoming*, art. 4, sec. 8; *Washington*, art. 3, sec. 12; *Montana*, art. 7, sec. 12; *Idaho*, art. 4, sec. 10; *United States Const.*, art. 1, sec. 7.

[4] Stimson's *Am. Statute Law*, sec. 277.

Dakota, South Dakota, Idaho, and Wyoming, the chief executive has the power of adjourning the legislature upon the failure of the two houses to agree as to the time of adjournment.[1]

All the constitutions except those of Massachusetts, Rhode Island, Vermont, and Wisconsin make it the duty of the executive to give the legislature information of the condition of the commonwealth, and to recommend such measures as he deems expedient.[2] Possessing extensive sources of information as to the advantages and defects of the laws, he can thus point out the evils and suggest the remedies. He may likewise in this manner lay before the legislature facts and information to assist it in its deliberations, and may thus be held responsible not only for the due administration of the existing system, but also for the means of improving it.[3]

In all commonwealths in which there is a lieutenant-governor, except Massachusetts and Rhode Island, that official is president of the senate with a casting vote.[4]

Besides this control over the legislature and legislation, the chief executive has, under all the constitutions, the power to grant pardons and commutations of sentence.[5] In New Hamp-

[1] Stimson's *Am. Statute Law*, sec. 278; *Const. of North Dakota*, sec. 75; *South Dakota*, art. 4, sec. 4; *Wyoming*, art. 4, sec. 4; *Washington*, art. 3, sec. 7; *Montana*, art. 7, sec. 2; *Idaho*, art. 4, sec. 9.

[2] Stimson's *Am. Statute Law*, sec. 280; *Const. of North Dakota*, sec. 75; *South Dakota*, art. 4, sec. 4; *Wyoming*, art. 4, sec. 4; *Washington*, art. 3, sec. 3; *Montana*, art. 3, sec. 10; *Idaho*, art. 4, sec. 8.

[3] Story's *Com. on the Const.*, vol. 2, p. 382.

[4] Stimson's *Am. Statute Law*, secs. 202, 282; *Const. of North Dakota*, sec. 77; *South Dakota*, art. 4, sec. 7; *Washington*, art. 3, sec. 6; *Montana*, art. 7, sec. 15; *Idaho*, art. 4, secs. 12 and 13; *Const. of United States*, art. 1, sec. 3. For the reason for this provision, see 2 Story, 307. There is no lieutenant-governor in Delaware, New Jersey, Georgia, Maryland, New Hampshire, Tennessee, Alabama, Maine, Arkansas, Oregon, and West Virginia.

[5] Stimson's *Am. Statute Law*, sec. 160; *Const. of North Dakota*, sec. 76; *South Dakota*, art. 4, sec. 5; *Wyoming*, art. 4, sec. 5; *Washington*, art. 3, sec. 9; *Montana*, art. 7, sec. 10.

shire, Massachusetts and Maine, he can only exercise this power with the advice and consent of a council; in Rhode Island, with the consent of the senate; and in Pennsylvania and Louisiana, upon the written recommendation of certain officers specified in the constitution. In Nevada, Florida, Connecticut, Idaho and Michigan, he is a member of a pardoning board, or court. In most instances he is powerless to pardon in cases of impeachment and treason.[1]

Upon conviction for treason he often has the power to suspend the execution of the sentence until the case can be reported to the legislature at its next meeting, when the legislature must either pardon or commute the sentence, direct the execution of the sentence, or grant a further reprieve.[2]

It would also seem to result from the principle on which the power of each branch of the legislature to punish for contempt is founded, that the executive cannot interpose in such a case. The main object of the power to punish for contempt is to secure a purity, independence and ability of the legislature adequate to the discharge of all its duties. If the executive should possess the power of pardoning persons in contempt, the legislature would be wholly dependent upon his good will and pleasure for the exercise of its own powers.[3]

In all commonwealths excepting Massachusetts, Rhode Island, New Hampshire, Connecticut, Vermont and Kansas, the governor has the power to grant reprieves.[4] In some commonwealths the power to pardon has been held to include the power to reprieve;[5] and in Maine, Vermont, New Jersey, Pennsylvania, Indiana, Iowa, Maryland, Delaware, Virginia, West Virginia,

[1] Stimson's *Am. Statute Law*, sec. 161; *Const. of Idaho*, art. 4, sec. 7; *United States Const.*, art. 2, sec. 2.

[2] See *Const. of New York*, art. iv, sec. 5.

[3] Story's *Com. on the Const.*, vol. 2, p. 337. As to the executive's power to pardon persons found guilty of contempt of court—see post.

[4] Stimson's *Am. Statute Law*, sec. 163.

[5] *Ex parte* Fleming, 60 Miss. 910.

Kentucky, Arkansas, Texas, Oregon, Nevada, South Carolina, Georgia, Alabama, Mississippi, Florida, Louisiana, and the newer commonwealths, the executive has the power to remit fines and forfeitures.[1]

Among powers judicial in their nature, exercised by one branch of the legislature generally, is that of impeachment. The constitution of Oregon expressly prohibits the impeachment of public officers.[2] The objection was raised in the National Convention of 1787 that the legislative power of impeachment violated the principle of the separation of governmental powers.[3] In Nebraska impeachments are tried by the judges of the supreme court, and in New York by the senate and the judges of the court of appeals. The constitutions of thirty-two commonwealths expressly specify that the governor is liable to impeachment,[4] and the constitutions of twenty-four that judicial officers may be impeached.[5]

In Maine, West Virginia, Nevada, South Carolina, Georgia, Mississippi, Florida, Wyoming and North Dakota, either house may punish any person not a member for disorderly or contemptuous conduct, such punishment not to extend beyond the final adjournment of the session.[6]

In confirming appointments made by the President of the United States, and in ratifying treaties, the Senate of the United States participates in the exercise of powers generally regarded

[1] Stimson's *Am. Statute Law*, sec. 64; *Const. of North Dakota*, sec. 76; *South Dakota*, art. 4, sec. 5; *Wyoming*, art. 4, sec. 5; *Washington*, art. 3, sec. 9; *Montana*, art. 7, sec. 10.

[2] Art. 1, sec. 19.

[3] See Story's *Com. on Const.*, vol. 2, p. 548.

[4] Stimson's *Am. Statute Law*, sec. 260; *Const. of North Dakota*, secs. 195, 196; *South Dakota*, art. 16, sec. 1; *Wyoming*, art. 3, sec. 17; *Washington*, art. 5, sec. 1; *Montana*, art. 5, sec. 15.

[5] *Const. of North Dakota*, sec. 197; *South Dakota*, art. 16, sec. 3; *Wyoming*, art. 3, sec. 18; *Washington*, art. 5, sec. 2; *Montana*, art. 5, sec. 17.

[6] Stimson's *Am. Statute Law*, sec. 276; *Const. of North Dakota*, sec. 48; *Wyoming*, art. 3, sec. 12.

as executive in their nature. In some commonwealths the legislature is given the power of appointing some of the important commonwealth officers. In New Jersey, the legislature, for example, appoints the treasurer and comptroller, in Delaware and Maryland the treasurer, in New Hampshire, Maine and Virginia, the treasurer and secretary, in Tennessee the comptroller, and in Maine the attorney-general.[1] The senate confirms the governor's appointment of the attorney-general and the secretary of state in New Jersey, of the superintendent of public works and prisons in New York, of the secretary of state and the attorney-general in Pennsylvania, and of the secretary of state in West Virginia, Kentucky, and Texas.[2] The constitutions of New Hampshire, Pennsylvania, Ohio, Indiana, Wisconsin, Kentucky, Nebraska, West Virginia, Kansas, Tennessee, Missouri, California, Oregon, Nevada, and Florida provide that officers whose appointment is not provided for by the constitution shall be appointed or elected in the manner prescribed by the legislature. In Rhode Island, Ohio, Wisconsin, Kansas, Virginia, West Virginia, North Carolina, California, Nevada, Illinois, New York, and Louisiana, the legislature is empowered to remove certain officers; and in Connecticut, Maryland, Delaware, Kentucky, Missouri, Texas, Oregon, South Carolina, Mississippi, Louisiana, New Hampshire, Massachusetts, Pennsylvania and Michigan, both houses of the legislature may address the governor to exercise his power of removal.[3] In West Virginia, Minnesota, Missouri, Nevada, Colorado, South Carolina, Texas, North Dakota, South Dakota, Wyoming, Washington, and Montana, the legislature may provide for the removal of inferior officers for malfeasance or misfeasance of their duties.[4]

Texas, Alabama, Louisiana, Tennessee, Indiana, Arkansas,

[1] Stimson's *Am. Statute Law*, sec. 202. [2] *Ibid.*, sec. 202. [3] *Ibid.*, sec. 265.

[4] *Ibid.*, secs. 210, 265, 268; *Const. of North Dakota*, sec. 197; *South Dakota*, art. 16, sec. 4; *Wyoming*. art. 3, sec. 19; *Washington*, art. 5, sec. 3; *Montana*, art. 5, sec. 18.

Mississippi, and Oregon permit their courts to remove certain officers, as the attorney-general.[1]

In Massachusetts, Maine, New Hampshire, Rhode Island, Colorado, and South Dakota, the judges of the supreme court are required, upon solemn occasions, upon the request of either house of the legislature, or of the governor and council, to give their opinions upon important questions of law: and in Florida they are required, upon the request of the governor, to give their opinions on any questions affecting his executive powers and duties.[2]

The opinions given in accordance with such constitutional requirements are generally held to be merely advisory, and not binding upon the courts in subsequent cases.[3]

The courts have declared that they will not construe and give their opinion on provisions which do not affect a pending act,[4] and which do not affect purely public rights.[5] In Massachusetts, the justices will not give an opinion on the proper construction of an existing act which the legislature may amend,[6] and in Colorado they will not answer questions covered by pending litigation.[7]

In Florida, the justices refused to render an opinion upon request of the governor, as to what character of a bill the legislature is denied the power to pass under a certain provision of the constitution, and which, when submitted to the governor, it will be his duty for that reason to disapprove, on the ground that such an opinion would not affect his executive but only his legislative powers and duties.[8]

In Missouri it has been said that while under provisions like the foregoing the governor may determine for himself

[1] Stimson's *Am. Statute Law*, sec. 267.

[2] Cooley's *Const. Limitations*, p. 53 n; *Const. of South Dakota*, art. 5, sec. 13

[3] See Thayer, *Memoranda on the Legal Effect of Opinions given by Judges*.

[4] In re Senate Resolutions, 21 Pac. Rep. 470. [5] *Ibid.*, 21 Pac. Rep. 478.

[6] Op. of Justices, 21 N. E. Rep. 439.

[7] In re Irrigation Resolution, 9 Col. 620. [8] Op. of Justices, 23 Fla. 297.

whether the occasion is such as to authorize him to call on the judges for their opinion, they must decide for themselves whether the occasion is such as to warrant the governor in making the call.[1]

In Delaware, the chancellor and judges, though not required by any constitutional provision to do so, gave, as a matter of courtesy, in response to a joint resolution of the general assembly, written opinions as to the power of that body to change the basis of the representation of the several counties in it.[2]

In Vermont there is a statute which provides that the governor may require an opinion on questions connected with the discharge of his duties, and in Kentucky an opinion has been given by the judges to the chief executive, without even the requirement of a statute, on the power of the governor to fill a vacancy in the supreme court.[3]

When President Washington, in 1793, requested the opinion of the judges of the United States supreme court upon the construction of the treaty of 1778 with France, they declined to give such an opinion.[4]

[1] Op. of Judges, 49 Mo. 216. The provision in the Missouri constitution of 1865 requiring the judges to give opinions in such cases was omitted from the constitution of 1875.

[2] Opinions of the Chancellor and Judges, Dover, 1883.

[3] Op. of Judges, 79 Ky. 621.

[4] 5 Marshall's *Life of Washington*, ch. 66, pp. 433–441.

CHAPTER VI

THE SEPARATION AND BALANCE OF POWERS IN THE TERRITORIES OF THE UNITED STATES

THE territories of the United States present an interesting form of local self-government. Their government is created by Congress acting pursuant to the Constitution, which provides: "The Congress shall have power to dispose of and make all needful rules and regulations respecting the territories or other property belonging to the United States."[1]

From this provision of the Constitution it follows that the political rights of the people of the territories are franchises which they hold as privileges in the legislative discretion of the Congress of the United States.[2] The form of government to be established therein depends exclusively on Congressional discretion. Having the power to erect territorial government, Congress may confer on it such powers, legislative, executive and judicial, as it deems best. It may confer upon it general legislative powers, subject only to the laws and the Constitution of the United States.

The power of Congress is such that it may not only abrogate laws of the territorial legislatures, but may itself legislate directly for the local government. It may make a void act of the territorial legislature valid, and a valid act void. In other words it has full and complete authority over the people of the territories, and all of the departments of the territorial governments. It may do for the territories what the people under the constitutions may do for the commonwealths.[3]

[1] Art. iv, sec. 3.

[2] Murphy *vs.* Ramsey, 114 U. S. 15, 45.

[3] National Bank *vs.* Yankton, 101 U. S. 129. See Burgess, *Pol. Sc. and Const. Law*, vol. 2, p. 159.

The relation of the territories to Congress very much resembles the former relation of the colonies to the British Parliament, the organic laws of the territories resembling the charters of the colonies. The organic laws of the territories take the place of the constitutions as the fundamental law of their local governments.[1]

Their organic laws have been construed in very much the same manner as corresponding clauses in the commonwealth constitutions have been. Thus it has been held that the legislative power conferred upon a territorial legislature by an organic act cannot be delegated;[2] that powers conferred upon the governor by such acts cannot be limited or restricted by the legislatures;[3] that territorial legislatures have only such powers as Congress bestows upon them.[4]

Although Congress might have governed the territories directly without the intervention of a local government, it has in most cases delegated the administrative power of governing the territories to local authorities created by it. By statute a government has been established for each of the territories, excepting Alaska and the Indian Territory, consisting of a legislative, executive and judicial department, with powers analogous to those vested in the governmental departments of the central and commonwealth governments of the United States.

Thus Congress has provided that the executive power of each territory shall be vested in a governor,[5] the legislative power in a governor and a legislative assembly consisting of a council and a house of representatives,[6] and the judicial power, in all territories except Arizona, in a Supreme Court, District Court, Probate Court and Justices of the Peace.[7] The judicial power in Arizona is vested in a Supreme Court and such

[1] National Bank *vs.* Yankton, 101 U. S. 129.

[2] Winter *vs.* Hughes, 3 Utah, 443.

[3] 16 Op. of Att'y-Gen'l, 27.

[4] Treadwell *vs.* Schnauber, 1 Dak. 236.

[5] *U. S. Rev. St.*, sec. 1841.

[6] *Ibid.*, sec. 1846.

[7] *Ibid.*, sec. 1907.

inferior courts as the legislative council may by law prescribe.[1] In some territories the judges are given the power to fix the time and place of holding courts,[2] which power some of the commonwealth courts regard as political or legislative.

The governors and chief justices are nominated, and by and with the advice and consent of the senate, appointed by the President of the United States.[3] The members of the legislature are elected by the qualified voters of the territories.[4]

The salaries of some of the judges are fixed by Congress.[5]

The governor is commander-in-chief of the militia of the territory. He is invested with the power of pardon. He may grant reprieves, remit fines and forfeitures for offences against the laws of the territories, and respites for offences against the laws of the United States, till the decision of the President can be made known thereon.[6] He also is invested with a limited veto power.[7]

The territorial legislatures are also expressly invested with the power to regulate and prescribe the manner in which judicial appeals are to be taken.

The laws passed by the legislatures of some of the territories must be submitted to Congress, and, if disapproved by it, they are to be null and void.[8]

The Constitution of the United States and such laws of the United States as are not locally inapplicable, have the same force and effect within all organized territories as elsewhere in the United States.[9]

Alaska and the Indian Territory are under the direct authority of the laws passed by Congress, and of officers appointed by the President, by and with the advice and consent of the senate.[10]

[1] *U. S. Rev. St.*, sec. 1908. [2] *Ibid.*, sec. 1915. [3] *Ibid.*, sec. 1897.

[4] *Ibid.*, sec. 1846. [5] *Ibid.*, sec. 1879. [6] *Ibid.*, sec. 1841.

[7] *Ibid.*, sec. 1842. [8] *Ibid.*, sec. 1850. [9] *Ibid.*, 1891.

[10] *Laws of 1884*, ch. 50.

As to Alaska, Congress has specially provided that there shall be no legislative assembly in the district.[1] The Secretary of the Interior is empowered to make all needful provisions for the education of children of school age therein, and the President is authorized to make such regulations as are necessary to carry out the provisions of the law in regard to the importation, manufacture and sale of distilled liquors.[2]

The courts have frequently been called upon to determine the exact nature of the territorial courts. It has been decided that they are to be deemed strictly territorial, and in no just sense constitutional courts in which the power conferred by the Constitution is deposited. They are purely territorial creations,[3] administrative bodies, and not courts of the United States;[4] and a territorial judge not being a constitutional, but only an administrative officer, is not regarded as liable to impeachment, but to suspension and removal by the President.[5]

The District of Columbia is governed pursuant to the constitution, which provides that Congress shall have power "to exercise exclusive legislation in all cases whatsoever, over such district (not exceeding ten square miles) as may by cession of particular States, and the acceptance of Congress, become the seat of government of the United States."[6] The legislative power thus given to Congress is direct, *exclusive* and absolute, and cannot be constitutionally delegated to any other body.[7] The administration of the government is committed to three

[1] *Laws of 1884*, ch. 53, sec. 9.

[2] As to the constitutionality of laws delegating powers of a legislative nature to the executive officers above named, see the Louisa Simpson, 2 Sawyer, 57.

[3] Burgess, *Pol. Sc. and Const. Law*, vol. 2, p. 332.

[4] American Ins. Co. *vs.* Canter, 1 Pet. 511; U. S. *vs.* Reynolds, 98 U. S. 145; Clinton *vs.* Englebrecht, 13 Wall. 434; U. S. *vs.* Guthrie, 17 How. 284.

[5] Howard *vs.* U. S., 22 Ct. of Cl. 305; McAllister *vs.* U. S., 141 U. S. 174.

[6] Art. 1, sec. 8, clause 17.

[7] Roach *vs.* Van Riswick, 4 MacArthur, 171; 15 Op. Att'y-Gen'l, 56. See also Eckloff *vs.* Dist. of Columbia, 4 Mackey, 572.

commissioners, appointed by the President. Concerning this government, Bryce in his "American Commonwealth" says, "strangely enough, though it is practically a despotism, it (Washington) is the best governed city in the country."[1]

[1] It has been proposed that Albany should be governed by the legislature of New York through a special committee of the legislature. See N. Y. Herald, Jan. 29, 1895.

CHAPTER VII

THE POWER OF THE COURTS TO DECLARE STATUTES UNCONSTITUTIONAL

THERE is no safeguard in the balancing of powers itself, which prevents the actual encroachment of one department, generally the legislative, upon the province of the other departments. Although an act of any department of government, beyond the scope of its constitutionally delegated power, must legally be regarded as a void act, yet the constitutions do not expressly indicate how or by whom it is to be determined whether any one of the departments or any agent of the government is actually infringing upon and assuming powers delegated to another department or agent of the government, or otherwise assuming unauthorized power. The assumption of this power by the courts in the United States has raised those tribunals to their unique and exalted position. The exercise of the power to declare statutes unconstitutional and void serves the courts as a shield of protection as a co-ordinate department of government, and serves the state as a balance-wheel between each of the departments. This power is to the courts what the veto is to the executive.

New Jersey, North Carolina, Rhode Island and Virginia each claim the distinction of priority in deciding this principle of our constitutional law.[1]

In New Jersey the question as to where this power was

[1] See Carson's *The Supreme Court of the United States*, p. 120; Cooley's *Const. Limitations*, chap. vii, p. 193, n.; Charles B. Elliott, "The Legislature and the Courts," *Political Science Quarterly*, vol. v, p. 224; *The Nation*, March 7, 1889; Sept. 28, 1893; Oct. 12, 1893; "Relation of the Judiciary to the Constitution," 19 *American Law Review*, 180.

vested was considered in 1779 in the case of Holmes against Walton, arising under what were then known as the Seizure Laws. The legislature enacted that trials under the above laws should be held before a jury of only six men. Notwithstanding that the court was then under legislative control, it held that this was an unconstitutional jury. The legislature acquiesced in the decision. It repealed that part of the act which related to the jury, and substituted a constitutional jury of twelve men in its place.[1]

In Virginia the question was raised, but not decided, as early as 1772, in the case of Robinson against Hardaway.[2]

In 1778 the legislature of Virginia passed a conditional act of attainder. It was never enforced; but it is uncertain whether the court refused to pass sentence under this law, and therefore put the person charged on trial according to the ordinary course of law,[3] or whether the act was not enforced on account of the voluntary action of the attorney-general.[4]

In 1782 an act passed by the legislature in 1776, taking from the executive his constitutional power of pardon, reached the courts.[5] The judge, without deciding the question at issue, said: "If the whole legislature—an event to be deprecated—should attempt to overleap the boundaries prescribed to them by the people, I, in administering the justice of the country, will meet the united powers at my seat in this tribunal, and pointing to the Constitution will say to them, 'Here is the limit of your authority; hither shall you go, but no further.'" The reporter's note to that case states that all the judges were of the opinion that the court had the power to

[1] Holmes *vs.* Walton, *Papers of American Historical Society*, vol. ii, p. 46. The case is referred to in State *vs.* Parkhurst, 4 Halstead, 444, and in Taylor *vs.* Reading, 4 Halstead (App.), 440.

[2] Jefferson's *Reports*, 109.

[3] Tucker's *Blackstone*, Appendix, p. 293.

[4] 4 Burk, 305.

[5] Commonwealth *vs.* Caton, 4 Call, 1. Rives' *Life of Madison*, vol. ii, p. 262 *et seq.*

declare any act of the legislature to be unconstitutional and void.

In 1788, the question was finally put to rest in that commonwealth by the interesting Case of the Judges.[1] The legislature had passed an act increasing the burdens of the judges. The judges in their remonstrances to the general assembly declared that the constitution and acts were in opposition, and could not exist together, and that the former must control the latter; that if this opinion needed any support, it could be found in the opinion of the legislators themselves, who had in several instances considered the constitution as prescribing limits to their powers as well as to those of the other departments of the government. To obviate the objection that the courts, while maintaining the independence of the judiciary, were encroaching upon the other departments, and assuming the right to control the legislature, it was observed that when the courts decided between an act of the people and an act of the legislature, they were within the line of their duty, declaring what the law is and not making a new law; and that, if the legislature should be disappointed, it could take an appeal to the people, who could exercise their original and supreme power whenever they thought proper to do so.[2]

In 1784 the mayor's court of New York City held the Trespass Act, authorizing owners to bring actions against those who occupied their houses under British orders during the British occupation, unconstitutional. The decision rested on the general principle that the act was against natural reason and justice.[3] Mass meetings were held in the city declaring such power most pernicious, and the assembly resolved such power would render legislation useless.[4]

[1] 4 Call, 135.

[2] This principle was reaffirmed in 1792 in Turner *vs.* Turner, 4 Call, 234, and in 1793 in Kempner *vs.* Hawkins, 2 Virginia Cases, 211.

[3] Rutgers *vs.* Waddington, Dawson's Pamphlet, 44. See Coxe, *Judicial Power and Unconstitutional Legislation*, p. 223.

[4] McMaster's *History of the People of the United States*, vol. i, pp. 219, 220.

In 1786 the legislature of Rhode Island passed an act to force people to accept paper money at its face value, and a penalty for refusing so to receive it was made collectible on summary conviction, without trial by jury. The court intimated that the act was void, because jury trial was assured by the Colonial Charter which then constituted the constitution of the commonwealth, but dismissed the case for want of jurisdiction. The law was repealed, but the judges were punished by a refusal of the legislature to re-elect them.[1]

The case of Bayard against Singleton reached the supreme court of North Carolina in 1786, at which time the judges comprising it had already asserted its authority to declare void and unconstitutional acts of the legislature. The court, however, held the case under advisement until 1787, when it declared the law then in question void, as destructive of trial by jury.

It was often difficult for men trained under the English system of jurisprudence to conceive the idea that a mere court should assume the prerogative of setting aside a law enacted by the legislature and approved by the executive.[2] This doctrine has met with great opposition in the Western States. In 1805 a law passed by the legislature of Ohio, extending the jurisdiction of the justices of the peace, was declared void.[3] Public clamor denounced this proceeding of the court as an unwarranted assumption of power. Two judges were impeached, but acquitted.[4] The doctrine was subsequently

[1] Trevett *vs.* Weeden; Arnold's *History of Rhode Island*, vol. ii, chap. 24, p. 525. Judge Cooley cites this as the first case which declared this principle; *Const. Limitations*, 6th edition, pp. 193, 194 n. In this he is followed by Prof. Bryce, *The American Commonwealth*, vol. i, p. 244. See *Pol. Sc. Quarterly*, vol. v, p. 234.

[2] Rogers' *Constitutional History of the United States*, p. 10.

[3] Case of Judge Pease. Cooley's *Const. Limitations*, p. 160 n.

[4] *West. Law Monthly*, June, 1863.

affirmed by the courts of that commonwealth without opposition.[1]

In Kentucky a legislative act which relieved the bank of the commonwealth from redeeming its notes in specie, was declared unconstitutional.[2] The legislature thereupon affirmed the constitutionality of the law. The issue of the election of 1824 was made to depend upon the right of the courts to annul a law passed by the representatives of the people. A majority, but not the required two-thirds of the House of Representatives, voted to impeach the judges. The legislature also repealed the law by which the court was organized, and enacted a law for the establishment of a new court. The courts held this act unconstitutional. This gave rise to two parties, the old and the new court parties. The old court party ultimately prevailed.[3]

As late as 1890 a decision of the Supreme Court of the United States, denying the legislature of Minnesota the power to fix railroad rates, aroused violent protests from the Farmers' Alliance. The Alliance passed resolutions declaring: "We call attention to the fact that the citizens of England, from whom we have largely derived our form of government, would not permit for one instant a bench of judges to nullify an act of parliament. No civilized government on earth has ever conferred such powers upon a court as are by our constitution granted to the United States Supreme Court. In our attempts to protect the rights of property, we have created a machine that threatens to destroy the rights of man."[4]

[1] Jordan *vs.* Dayton, 4 Ohio, 294, decided in 1829.

[2] Lapsley *vs.* Breashear, 4 Litt. 47.

[3] Collins' *History of Kentucky*, vol. i, pp. 218, 222.

[4] *Pol. Sc. Quarterly*, vol. v, pp. 248, 369. In Switzerland, the only existing republican state, besides the United States, with a federal form of government, the cantonal courts have not, except in Uri, the power to declare invalid a law enacted by a cantonal legislature. Swiss Federal Const. of 1874, arts. 102, 110, 114. See Dub's "Das oeffentliche Recht der Zweizerischen Eidgenossenschaft," Pt. 1, p. 113.

The power of the United States courts to declare statutes unconstitutional and void, was in due time asserted by the Supreme Court of the United States. In March, 1792, Congress by law directed the various circuit courts of the United States to pass upon the validity of pension claims, but subjected their decisions to review by the Secretary of War, and finally to revision by Congress. The judges of the circuit court for the district of Pennsylvania addressed a letter to the President, declaring that they could not proceed under the act because the business directed was not of a judicial nature, and because the judgment of the court would be controlled by the legislature or by an executive officer, which would be inconsistent with the independence of the judicial power which was vested in the courts.[1] The judges of the circuit court for New York unanimously agreed that it was the duty of each branch of the government to abstain from and oppose encroachments by any department upon either of the others; that the duties assigned by the act were not judicial, and that by the Constitution neither the Secretary of War nor other executive officer, nor any legislative authority, could sit as a court of errors on the judicial acts or opinions of the courts. But, taking into consideration the benevolent object of the act, they agreed to execute it as commissioners. The circuit court for North Carolina sent like remonstrances to the Presi-

[1] More recently the United States Supreme Court has held for quite similar reasons that it cannot be granted jurisdiction to review the action of the Court of Claims in respect to a claim examined and allowed in the latter court under an act of Congress, under which neither the Court of Claims nor the Supreme Court could do any more than certify their opinion to the Secretary of the Treasury, and under which, whether the claim was paid or not did not depend upon the decision of the court, but upon the future action of the Secretary of the Treasury and of Congress. Gordon *vs.* U. S, 117 U. S. 697. See In re Sanborn, 148 U. S. 222; DeGroot *vs.* U. S., 5 Wall. 419. The Constitution of North Carolina gives the court original jurisdiction over claims against the government, but provides that its hearings shall be merely recommendatory, and that its decision shall be reported to the next general assembly for its action.—Art. iv, sec. 11. See Bledsoe *vs.* State, 64 N. C. 392.

dent. Judge Wilson, however, refused to act even as a commissioner. Shortly thereafter, William Hayburn petitioned for a mandamus to compel the circuit court for Pennsylvania to proceed under the act of Congress and to pass upon the validity of his pension claim.[1] As the legislature provided another means for the relief of pensioners while the court held the above motion under advisement, no decision was ever pronounced.

The new act imposed upon the Secretary of War and Attorney-General the duty to obtain an adjudication of the Supreme Court upon the validity of the pensions allowed by the determination of certain persons who styled themselves commissioners under the act of 1792. An amicable action was therefore brought by the United States against Yale Todd. The judges of the Supreme Court were unanimously of the opinion that the power given to the circuit courts as courts could not be construed to be given to the judges out of court, as commissioners. They held the act unconstitutional because it imposed non-judicial functions on the judiciary, and decided that the judges had not the right voluntarily to proceed under the act as commissioners.[2]

In 1795 a United States circuit court held unconstitutional the Quieting and Confirming Act of Pennsylvania, relative to her controversy with Connecticut as to the title to certain lands. The court declared that every act of the legislature repugnant to the Constitution is absolutely void. If a legislative act impugns a constitutional provision, the former must give way. In such case it will be the duty of the court to adhere to the Constitution and to declare the act null and void.[3] Although this opinion had been repeatedly reaffirmed,[4] yet as

[1] Hayburn's Case, and note, 2 Dallas, 409.

[2] United States *vs*. Fereira, 13 Howard, 52 n.

[3] Van Horn's Lessee *vs*. Dorrance, 2 Dall. 304.

[4] United States *vs*. Villato, 2 Dall. 370, 1797; Hylton *vs*. United States, 3 Dall, 171, 1796; Calder *vs*. Bull, 3 Dall. 386, 1798.

late as 1800 Mr. Justice Chase declared: "Although it is alleged all acts of the legislature in direct opposition to the Constitution are void, still it is a question where the power resides to declare them void."[1]

Therefore, *notwithstanding* the case of United States *vs.* Todd, this question might still have been considered an open one when it came before the Supreme Court in 1803, involved as it was in the case of Marbury against Madison.[2]

By means of a remorseless logic from which there can be no escape, Chief Justice Marshall shivered into atoms any pretensions of Congress to override the Constitution. In an opinion which cannot be abridged, or too frequently quoted, he says: "The question whether an act repugnant to the constitution can become the law of the land, is a question deeply interesting to the United States; but happily not of an intricacy proportioned to its interest. It seems only necessary to recognize certain principles supposed to have been long and well established, to decide it.

"That the people have an original right to establish for their future government such principles as in their opinion shall most conduce to their own happiness, is the basis on which the whole American fabric has been erected. . . .

"The original supreme will organizes the government and assigns to the different departments their respective powers. It may either stop here, or establish certain limits not to be transcended by those departments. . . .

"The powers of the legislature are defined and limited; and that those limits may not be mistaken or forgotten, the constitution is written. To what purpose are powers limited, and to what

[1] Cooper *vs.* Telfair, 4 Dall. 19.

[2] 1 Cranch, 137. It may be interesting to observe that Marshall studied law under Chancellor George Wythe, who gave expression to the opinion of the court in the case of Commonwealth *vs.* Caton (*ante*, p. 53), and that Judge Iredell, one of the associate justices of the Supreme Court, concurring in the decision of Marbury *vs.* Madison, was counsel for the plaintiff in the case of Bayard *vs.* Singleton. (See *ante*, p. 55.)

purpose is that limitation committed to writing, if those limits may at any time be passed by those intended to be restrained?

"The constitution is either a superior paramount law, unchangeable by ordinary means, or it is on a level with ordinary legislative acts, and like any other act is alterable when the legislature shall please to alter it.

"If the former part of the alternative be true, then a legislative act contrary to the constitution is not law. If the latter part be true, then written constitutions are absurd attempts on the part of the people to limit a power in its own nature illimitable.

"Certainly all those who have framed written constitutions, contemplate them as forming the fundamental and paramount law of the nation, and consequently the theory of every such government must be, that an act of the legislature repugnant to the constitution is void.

"This theory is essentially attached to a written constitution, and is consequently to be considered by this court as one of the fundamental principles of society. It is not, therefore, to be lost sight of in the further consideration of this subject.

"If an act of the legislature repugnant to the constitution is void, does it, notwithstanding its invalidity, bind the courts and oblige them to give it effect? Or, in other words, though it be not law, does it constitute a rule as operative as though it was a law? This would be to overthrow in fact what was established in theory; and would seem at first view an absurdity too gross to be insisted upon.

"It shall, however, receive a more attentive consideration. It is emphatically the province and duty of the judicial department to say what the law is. Those who apply the rule to particular cases must of necessity expound and interpret that rule. If two laws conflict with each other, the courts must decide upon the operation of each. So if a law be in opposition to the constitution; if both the law and the constitution apply to a particular case, so that the court must either decide that case conformably to the law, disregarding the constitution, or conformably to the constitution, disregarding the law—the court must determine which of these conflicting rules governs the case. This is of the very essence of judicial duty.

"If, then, the courts are to regard the constitution, and the constitution is superior to any ordinary act of the legislature, the constitution, and not such ordinary act, must govern the case to which they both apply, Those, then, who controvert the principle that the constitution is to be considered in court as a paramount law, are reduced to the necessity of maintaining that courts must close their eyes on the constitution and see only the law."

This opinion established the principle upon a legal basis which cannot be shaken.[1]

Lieber says, "The court does not decide upon the doings of the legislature. It simply decides for the case in hand whether there actually are conflicting laws, and if so, which is the higher law that demands obedience, when both may not be obeyed at the same time. As however the decision becomes the leading decision for all future cases of the same import, until indeed legitimate and proper authority reverses it, the question of constitutionality is virtually decided, and it is decided in a natural, easy, legitimate and safe manner, according to the principle of the supremacy of a law, and the dependence of justice."[2]

Nor does this construction imply a superiority of the judicial to the legislative power. It only implies that the power of the people is superior to both, and that where the will of the legislature declared in its statute stands in opposition to

[1] See also Cohen *vs.* Virginia, 6 Wheaton, 264, and Fletcher *vs.* Peck, 6 Cranch, 87; *Federalist*, nos. 22, 78, 80-82; Webster on the "Independence of the Judiciary," *Webster's Works*, vol. iii, p. 29. See 131 U. S, Appendix, p. 235, for list of cases in which Supreme Court has held statutes void. See, for comment upon this list, Coxe, *Judicial Power and Unconstitutional Legislation*. This author maintains that the Constitution of the United States was intended to confer, and does expressly confer, authority upon the courts to determine legislation to be unconstitutional.

[2] Lieber's *Civil Liberty and Self-Government.*

the will of the people declared in the constitution, the judges ought to be governed by the latter rather than by the former.[1]

Notwithstanding the firmness with which the foregoing principle has been established, it would be error to infer that the courts are the only, or, in every case, the ultimate interpreters of the constitution.[2]

Every department of government invested with certain constitutional powers, must in the first instance be the judge of its powers under the constitution, or it could not act.[3] So, if a department is required to act in a case not hitherto settled by any proper authority, such department must in the first instance decide for itself whether, consistently with the constitution, the act can be done.

In many cases the decisions of the executive and the legislative departments become final and conclusive, being from their very nature incapable of revision. Thus as matters exclusively of a political or discretionary character belong to the legislative and executive departments, they cannot be examined elsewhere.[4] Under a constitutional provision that "In all cases

[1] Bates *vs.* Kimball, 2 Chipp, 77.

[2] Soon after the adoption of the United States Constitution, several commonwealths contended that each commonwealth had a right to judge for itself as well of the infractions of that Constitution as of the mode and measure of redress. See *Virginia Resolutions of 1798; Kentucky Resolutions of 1797, 1799.* But subsequent events have established too firmly to admit of doubt that the United States Supreme Court, and not any commonwealth, or its agencies, is the ultimate tribunal to determine whether laws of Congress, or of the commonwealth legislatures, or decisions of the commonwealth courts, are in conflict with the Constitution of the United States. Dodge *vs.* Woolsey, 18 How. 331; Martin *vs.* Hunter's Lessee, 1 Wheat. 304; Story's *Com. on the Const.*, vol. 1, pp. 228, 275; *North American Review,* Oct., 1830, p. 500.

[3] Kendall *vs.* Inhabitants of Kingston, 5 Mass. 524.

[4] See Luther *vs.* Borden, 7 How. 1; Cherokee Nation *vs.* Georgia, 5 Peters, 1; Mississippi *vs.* Johnston, 4 Wallace, 475; Georgia *vs.* Stanton, 6 Id. 50. Certainly the court must, when called upon to do so, itself finally determine when the case is one primarily affecting private rights and private property, and when, on the contrary, it is primarily a political question. Burgess, *Pol. Sc. and Const. Law,* vol. 2, p. 327. The court finally determines whether it may review the action of the other departments.

where a general law can be made applicable, no special law shall be enacted," it is well settled that the legislature has the ultimate power to determine the cases in which special laws may constitutionally be passed.[1] Where the constitution empowers the executive to convene the legislature on extraordinary occasions, he alone is the judge as to whether extraordinary occasions within the meaning of the constitution have arisen, and neither the legislative department nor the judicial department can intervene to compel or enjoin action.[2]

In taking care that the laws be faithfully executed, it may become necessary for the executive to interpret the true meaning of the constitution and of statutes.[3] If no proper case for the judicial revision of his interpretation of the constitution, or even of a statute, can be framed, and the legislature cannot override the veto which the executive may put in the way of revising his interpretation, the executive's interpretation becomes in fact ultimate. His construction of a law, and his decision as to its constitutionality, is binding upon and must be followed by his subordinates. So, where a governor held a provision in a law, exempting certain persons under certain conditions from a tax, unconstitutional, and directed the tax to be levied on the property sought to be exempted, it was held that his subordinates must act accordingly.[4]

Whenever the executive or legislative departments are called

[1] State *vs.* Hitchcock, 1 Kan. 178. See State *vs.* Boone City Court, 50 Mo. 317; Patterson *vs.* Barlow, 60 Pa. St. 54; Malory *vs.* Henrietta, 11 Ohio St. 636.

[2] Cooley's *Const. Limitations*, p. 55. See In re State Censor, 21 Pac. R. 477; Whitman *vs.* R. R. Co., 2 Harr. (Del.) 514; Martin *vs.* Mott, 12 Wheat. 19.

[3] See United States *vs.* Lytle, 5 McLean, 9; State *vs.* Hallock, 16 Mo. 373; Castro *vs.* De Uriarte, 16 Fed. Rep., 93. The Revenue Act of Aug. 24, 1894, contains a paragraph providing for the refunding of the internal revenue tax paid on alcohol used in the arts. The executive department concluded that it would be impossible to carry out its provisions without further legislation, and accordingly the rebate on this tax has never been paid.

[4] State *vs.* Buchanan, 24 W. Va. 362. See U. S. *vs.* Marble, 3 Mackey, 32; State *vs.* Kelsey, 44 N. J. L. 1.

upon to act, they may construe the constitution for themselves to the extent of abstaining from exercising a power because they deem its exercise unconstitutional, even though the courts have declared it a constitutional assumption of power. On the other hand, acts and powers, the assumption of which the courts have declared unconstitutional, the departments ought to abstain from exercising, because the state has established and ordained the courts, as its agent, to determine the extent of the powers granted to the departments. In other words, the departments may refrain from exercising powers which the court has considered constitutional because, they deem them unconstitutional, but should not exercise a power which the court has declared unconstitutional because they deem it constitutional; that is, the departments may properly consider themselves entitled to less power than the court would grant them, but not to greater powers. In this sense the departments may ultimately construe the constitution, and treat as unconstitutional an act which the courts declare constitutional; but they never properly exercise the power to declare constitutional what the courts declare unconstitutional.[1]

Thus President Jackson acted within the spirit of the Constitution when, in opposition to the decision of the United States Supreme Court, maintaining the constitutionality of the act establishing the Bank of the United States, he vetoed a bill providing for a re-charter of the Bank, because he considered it unconstitutional, notwithstanding the decision of the court

[1] The same person who as a legislator would refrain from supporting a proposed law because he considered that it would be unconstitutional, may as a judge feel compelled to declare it constitutional, on account of judicial precedent. Mr. White as a member of Congress refused to support the Income Tax Law of August 24, 1894, because he thought it unconstitutional, notwithstanding any possible decision of the courts to the contrary. When afterwards the question of its constitutionality was presented to him as one of the justices of the Supreme Court, he declared it constitutional. Pollock *vs.* Farmers' Loan & Trust Co., 157 U. S. 429, 158 Id. 601.

to the contrary. But, the language which he used in justification of his action is too general to be entirely correct. In the course of his veto message he said: "It is maintained by the advocates of the bank that its constitutionality in all its features ought to be considered as settled by precedent and by the decision of the Supreme Court. To this conclusion I cannot assent. . . . . . The opinion of the Supreme Court ought not to control the co-ordinate authorities of this government. The Congress, the Executive and the Court must each for itself be guided by its own opinion of the constitution. Each public officer who takes an oath to support the constitution swears that he will support it as he understands it. It is as much the duty of the House of Representatives, of the Senate, and of the President to decide upon the constitutionality of any bill or resolution which may be presented to them for passage or approval as it is of the Supreme Judges, when it may be brought before them for judicial decision. The opinion of the judges has no more authority over Congress than the opinion of Congress has over the judges, and on that point the President is independent of both.

"The authority of the Supreme Court must not, therefore, be permitted to control Congress or the Executive when acting in their legislative capacity, but to have only such influence as the force of their reasoning may deserve."

The President having been empowered to veto acts of the legislature, in his own discretion, he can give as the reason for the exercise of his discretion the fact that he deems the proposed law unconstitutional, though the courts have held a similar act constitutional.[1]

[1] President Lincoln, referring to the decision in the Dred Scott Case, in his inaugural speech, said: "I do not forget the position assumed by some that constitutional questions are to be decided by the Supreme Court, nor do I deny that such decision must be binding in any case on the parties to a suit—as to the object of that suit—while they are entitled to very high respect and consideration by all the other departments of the government. . . .

"At the same time the candid citizen must confess that if the policy of the

So, likewise, if the President is called upon to pardon a person imprisoned under a law, whether summarily or after a trial in which the validity of the law was asserted, he may grant the pardon, because he deems the law unconstitutional, even though the courts have declared it constitutional. Thus, Jefferson undoubtedly acted within his authority when he pardoned persons imprisoned under the alien and sedition laws, because he considered them unconstitutional. In justifying his action, however, he used language which the occasion did not require. He said, "Each department of the government is truly independent of the others, and has an equal right to decide for itself what is the meaning of the constitution in the laws submitted to its action, and especially when it is to act ultimately and without appeal."[1]

This statement is erroneous. In all cases, except those of a political or discretionary character, like those above referred to, the decisions of the courts ought to be regarded as binding on the other departments of government, because the court, in all other cases, was intended as the final expositor of the constitution. Were the President, because he thought the decision of a court unconstitutional, to refuse or to prevent the enforcement of its judgment in a case in which his assistance is needed, he would in effect be sitting as a court of appeals, assuming the judicial power vested by the constitution in the courts.

In the history of our country the judgments of the courts have failed to receive the proper recognition of the executive on at least two occasions.

During Jackson's administration, the Supreme Court de-

government upon vital questions affecting the people is to be irrevocably fixed by the decisions of the Supreme Court, the instant they are made in ordinary litigation between parties in personal actions, the people will have ceased to be their own rulers, having to that extent practically resigned their government into the hands of that eminent tribunal."

[1] 4 *Correspondence*, 316, 317.

clared a law of Georgia forbidding white persons to reside within the land of the Cherokee Nation unconstitutional, and ordered Worcester, a missionary, who had been imprisoned under it, to be released.[1] Georgia would not obey, and Jackson would not enforce obedience. He is reported to have said, "John Marshall has made his decision, now let him enforce it."[2]

At the outbreak of the rebellion in 1861, one Merryman, suspected of treason, was arrested by a military officer, and placed in confinement at Fort McHenry. Chief Justice Taney issued a writ of habeas corpus to the officer who had Merryman in charge. The officer refused to obey the writ on the ground that the President had authorized him to suspend it. On account of the danger of a conflict with the executive who, with the acquiescence of the nation, had assumed despotic war powers, the Chief Justice took no further action beyond filing an opinion to the effect that the privileges of the writ could not be suspended except by act of Congress.[3]

While the reconstruction of certain commonwealths was going on, after the rebellion, Congress so shaped its legislation that the Supreme Court had no opportunity to pass upon the validity of the Re-construction Acts. As the original jurisdiction of the court is limited, and as its appellate jurisdiction is by the Constitution subject to such exceptions and regulations as Congress shall provide,[4] Congress, fearing an adverse decision on appeal in a case then pending, involving the constitutionality of those acts, repealed the statute under which the appeal was taken and thus compelled the court to dismiss it.[5]

In every case in which the executive for any reason whatsoever refuses to enforce the judgment of the court, he is

[1] Worcester *vs.* Georgia, 6 Pet. 515.

[2] Von Holst, *Const. History*, vol. 1750–1832, p. 458.

[3] See Merryman's Case, Taney, 246.

[4] *Ex parte* Yerger, 8 Wall. 85; The Lucy, 8 Wall. 307.

[5] See McCardle's Case, 7 Wall. 506.

guilty of a violation of the constitution, and is responsible primarily to the legislature, and ultimately to that great tribunal to which each department is responsible, the people.[1]

[1] See Story, *Com. on the Const.*, vol. 1, p. 273; vol. 2, p. 391; Cooley's *Const. Limitations*, p. 68; "Are the Departments of Government Independent?" *Am. L. Rev.*, March, 1887.

PART II

CHAPTER VIII

RESTRICTED MEANING OF THE TERMS LEGISLATIVE, EXECUTIVE AND JUDICIAL IN THE DISTRIBUTING CLAUSE.

ALTHOUGH the three chief governmental powers of the central and commonwealth governments are vested in three distinct and independent departments, what are legislative, executive or judicial powers within the meaning of the distributing clause, is not defined or expressed in any of the constitutions. The boundary line between them is undefined and often difficult to determine.[1]

As the succeeding pages will show, the courts, when called upon to determine the exact meaning of the distributing clause, have often construed it as though it provided that powers legislative in their nature are vested in the legislature, powers executive in their nature in the executive department of government, and powers judicial in their nature in the courts; and that the legislature shall never assume powers judicial or executive in their nature, nor the executive department powers legislative or judicial in their nature, nor the judicial department powers legislative or executive in their nature. It must, however, be self-evident that no clear distinction can be based upon the nature of the powers to be exercised by the different departments.

[1] State *vs.* Peters, 43 Ohio St. 629. In the New Hampshire Constitution (pt. ii) an effort has been made to define legislative power, but not with much success.

Any act which *in effect* establishes a rule of civil conduct irrespective of the manner in which, or the body by which, it is enacted, must be conceded to be legislative in its nature. Of such nature are not only the laws passed by Congress and the commonwealth legislatures, but also the rules of practice and the common law principles established by the decisions of courts and the rules and regulations established by the executive department in the exercise of its delegated ordinance power.

Powers legislative in their nature are also exercised by various bodies and officers, not belonging to either of the three departments of government, such as the municipal council or other legislative body of a city or village, and the officers having the general control of county affairs, styled in some commonwealths supervisors, in others county commissioners, and in still others chosen freeholders.[1]

Any act which tends, no matter how indirectly, to the enforcement of a law, or the enforcement of a superior command, is executive in its nature.

Powers conceded by theoretical writers to be executive in their nature would not only include the powers exercised by the executive department, but also many powers actually exercised by the legislative and judicial departments, in many cases necessarily, in order to insure their independence.

Each one of the three departments must have some appointing power as an incident of its principal power, for without it no department can be independent. Where an appointment is essential to the proper exercise of a judicial duty, the court concerned has authority to make it.[2] Likewise, legislative bodies may elect or appoint officers of their respective branches and relative to their department of government.[3]

[1] Waugh *vs.* Chauncey, 13 Cal. 11; People *vs.* Carpenter, 24 N. Y. 86.

[2] State *vs.* Smith, 15 Mo. App. 412; In re Janitor, 35 Wis. 410, relating to the power of a court to appoint its own janitor; State *vs.* Noble, 118 Ind. 350.

[3] State *vs.* Hyde, 121 Ind. 20; Tenney *vs.* State, 27 Wis. 388.

Powers executive in their nature are also often exercised by administrative officers, or bodies not belonging to either the legislative, judicial or even executive department of government provided for by the constitution.[1]

Power to hear and to determine, or power to ascertain facts and to apply the law to the facts when ascertained, is judicial in its nature.

Powers of such a nature are not only exercised by the courts, but also by the legislative and executive departments, and by various administrative bodies and officers not belonging to either of the three foregoing departments.

All departments alike inquire into facts and proceed upon them. Facts are or should be the basis of legislation as well as of judgment, and when there is a doubt or controversy concerning them, the considerate legislator stays his hand until they have been ascertained. So far as the process is concerned, that of the legislator and that of the judge are the same; the difference lies in the use to which the facts are put when found.[2]

The powers exercised by the legislature in authorizing the sale of lands of persons resting under legal disabilities, and in granting divorces by special laws, are conceded to be judicial in their nature. Of such nature must be presumed to be the power exercised by the legislature in passing upon the validity of claims against the government, and in determining contested election cases.[3]

The power of removal for cause, often vested in the executive, is judicial in its nature.

[1] State *vs.* Barbour, 53 Conn. 76; Achley's Case, 4 Abb. Pr. 35, which holds that the power conferred upon the common council of a city to appoint to office is executive, and in no sense legislative, and therefore not subject to the veto power of the mayor.

[2] *Ex parte* Shrader, 33 Cal. 279. See Watkins *vs.* Holman, 16 Pet. 25; Miners' Bk. *vs.* U. S., Green (Ia.), 553.

[3] See State *vs.* Harmon, 31 Ohio St. 250.

The proceedings before the interstate commerce commission, which like the courts regularly publishes its reports, and before the various commonwealth commissions and boards, are of a judicial nature.[1] Assessors in the valuation of property for taxation,[2] town boards of equalization in determining the value of lands,[3] commissioners appointed to determine and award damages for property taken by virtue of the right of eminent domain,[4] municipal boards authorized to hear and determine claims,[5] county commissioners in passing upon claims against the county,[6] school officers in deciding upon the removal of a teacher, or the expulsion of a scholar,[7] police boards disciplining a member of the police force by reprimand, forfeiture, withholding of the salary, or dismissal,[8] county commissioners in deciding upon the application for a permit to sell intoxicating liquors, and inspectors of elections and boards of registration in deciding upon the existence of the necessary qualifications of a voter,[9] exercise powers judicial in their nature. All hear and determine questions in the exercise of their functions more or less directly affecting private as well as public rights.[10]

Besides each one of the departments exercising powers in their nature legislative, executive and judicial, there are many administrative officers in every commonwealth vested with like powers.[11]

[1] *Ex parte* Shrader, 33 Cal. 279.
[2] Williams *vs.* Weaver, 75 N. Y. 30.
[3] Steele *vs.* Dunham, 26 Wis. 393.
[4] Van Steenbergh *vs.* Bigelow, 3 Wend. 42.
[5] Wall *vs.* Trumbull, 16 Mich. 228.
[6] B'd of Com'rs *vs.* Gregory, 42 Ind. 32.
[7] Stephenson *vs.* Hall, 14 Barb. 222.
[8] *Laws of N. Y.*, 1882, ch. 410, sec. 272.
[9] Fausler *vs.* Parsons, 6 W. Va. 486.

[10] As to the constitutionality of vesting these administrative powers, judicial in their nature, in officers other than judicial, see Keely *vs.* Pittsburgh, 104 U. S. 78; Hagar *vs.* Reclamation District, 111 U. S. 701; Weimer *vs.* Bunbery, 30 Mich. 201; McMillen *vs.* Anderson, 95 U. S. 37. These cases decide that administrative process of the customary sort is as much due process of law as judicial process.

[11] See Waugh *vs.* Chauncey, 13 Cal. 11.

Judge Cooley, in writing about the classification of public officers, says, "The duties imposed upon officers are supposed to be capable of classification under one of these heads, the legislative, executive or judicial, and to pertain accordingly to one of the three departments of government designated by those names. But the classification cannot be very exact, and there are numerous officers who cannot be classified at all under these heads. The reasons will be apparent if we name one class as an illustration. Taxing officers perform duties which in strictness are neither executive nor judicial, though in some particulars they merely execute the orders of superiors, and in others they judge for themselves what is to be done. But sometimes also their duties partake of the legislative character. All such officers are usually called administrative, while inferior executive officers are designated ministerial."[1]

The revised statutes of New York of 1830 classified officers within the commonwealth as legislative officers, executive officers, judicial officers, and administrative officers. "The powers of such administrative officers as supervisors and county commissioners are sometimes legislative, sometimes judicial, and sometimes executive in their nature. They cannot be classed consistently under any particular head; and so these officers are allowed to perform the duties enjoined upon them by law, without any nice examination into the character of the powers conferred."[2] "The board of supervisors is a special tribunal with mixed powers, administrative, legislative, and judicial."[3] "Judicial powers are often conferred upon officers whose general functions are executive or ministerial; and

[1] *The Southern Law Rev.*, vol. 3 (N. S.) 531. Administrative officers may be ministerial officers. It would therefore be advisable to employ the term administrative as indicated hereafter. The term ministerial should be used only in contradistinction to discretionary or judicial.

[2] State *vs.* Com'rs, 7 Nev. 392; People *vs.* El Dorado, 8 Cal. 58.

[3] United States *vs.* Arredendo, 6 Pet. 691, 729.

merely executive or ministerial functions are often conferred upon those whose general functions are judicial. So executive, ministerial, or even judicial powers are often conferred upon a body of officers whose general functions are legislative."[1]

These illustrations will suffice to show that either the constitutions have been violently disregarded in the union of all the powers in each one of the departments, and in certain administrative officers, or that the distinction between the departments was not intended to be based upon differences existing in the nature of the powers to be exercised by each department.

That no separation of powers, based upon the nature of the different governmental powers, was ever intended to be inserted in our organic law, would convincingly appear from a most cursory perusal of the debates in the constitutional conventions.

The framers of our constitutions provided for the organization of three great departments of government: the legislature, consisting of a comparatively great number of individuals; the judiciary, consisting of a comparatively small number of individuals; and the executive department, consisting generally of one individual, or a certain number of individuals expressly specified in the constitution as being members of the executive department of the government.

Familiar with the theory of Montesquieu, but unfamiliar with any supposed possibility of classifying powers according to their intrinsic nature, they vested legislative power, meaning thereby only the power of enacting general laws for the entire government, in the legislature; judicial power, meaning thereby only the power of determining and protecting the rights of persons under the constitution and constitutional laws, in the courts; and executive power, meaning thereby the power of seeing that the laws are faithfully executed, in the executive department.

Next they considered, in the light of the experience of past

[1] Throop's *Law of Public Officers*, sec. 25.

governments, other important powers which they thought their government in the course of its existence would probably be called upon to exercise. They did not enter into a philosophical discussion as to whether such a power was legislative, executive or judicial in its nature, but deliberated in which one or more of the departments already established by them the given power could with greatest propriety and safety be vested. Certain governmental powers, either because they were not considered of sufficient importance, or because the proper exercise thereof was supposed to require technical knowledge, or because the departments already established were not deemed properly adapted to their exercise, they vested in a governmental agency specially created for the purpose, and which did not form part of either of the three great departments.

Powers which would require promptitude, activity, decision, or unity of plan, if of sufficient importance, they vested in the executive. For instance, for such reason, they made the President of the United States commander-in-chief of the army and navy of the United States, and of the militia of the several commonwealths when called into the actual service of the United States.[1]

Considering the necessity in every humane government of a power of tempering, in extreme cases, legal justice with mercy, the importance and the liability to abuse of such a power, and the impracticability of a continuous session of the legislature, they vested the pardoning power in the executive. To the objection that such a provision would invest the executive with power judicial in its nature, they gave little attention[2].

They did not waste time in discussing whether the power of receiving ambassadors could be considered executive, legislative, or judicial; but, observing that in all foreign governments this power was exercised by the executive department, and taking into consideration the dignity of the office, they vested the power in the President.[3]

[1] See Story's *Com. on the Const.*, vol. 2, p. 338. [2] *Ibid.*, p. 330. [3] *Ibid.*, p. 383.

Had the constitutional convention tried to determine whether the treaty-making power was executive or legislative in its nature, with a view to vest it accordingly, they would have found that from one point of view, the manner of its exercise, it would be considered historically as well as theoretically, executive; from another point of view, that of its effect, as legislative.[1]

Considering the secrecy and dispatch which may be necessary to the making of a treaty, and the want of secrecy and tendency to delay incident to assemblies, they vested the treaty-making power in the executive; but fearing the liability to abuse of this great power, they subjected it to the deliberative assent of two-thirds of the Senate.[2]

Having premised the foregoing, we are now in a position to understand the true and only meaning which can be ascribed to the distributing clause, and also to understand how irrelevant

[1] This example shows the impossibility of basing any distinctions upon the nature of powers. Just as one governmental power may be both executive and legislative in its nature, so a power may be both judicial and legislative in its nature. In designating a power as judicial, we generally refer to the mode of its exercise; in speaking of a power as legislative, we often refer to its effect.

Had a distinction according to the nature of powers been intended, insurmountable difficulties would have been encountered in the attempt to define the distinctive elements. The confusion which would result must be evident to those who are familiar with the law regarding writs, especially those of certiorari and mandamus, and the law regarding exemption from responsibility of officers for legislative and judicial acts. Acts considered legislative, executive or judicial, when exercised by one body, are considered to be of a different nature when exercised by another body, or even by the same body for different purposes. Acts regarded as of a special nature when reviewed by the courts for one purpose, as, for example, in order to determine the propriety of granting the writ of mandamus, are regarded by the courts as being of an entirely different nature when reviewed by the courts for another purpose, as, for example, in order to determine the responsibility of an officer for his acts.

Indeed, the decisions of the courts cannot be reconciled to any formula or general principle or definition. Every case must stand on its own merits, unless an exact precedent can be found.

[2] See Story's *Com. on the Const.*, vol. 2, p. 346.

it is for the courts to discuss the nature of powers, in deciding upon the constitutional exercise of power, and how erroneous are some of the decisions which have been based upon distinctions as to the nature of the powers exercised.[1]

The general clause, vesting legislative power in the legislature, vests therein only the power of enacting general laws for the entire government. Besides this, the constitutions specially vest many other powers in the legislature, such as the power of impeachment, and of removal in certain cases. Any and every power vested in the legislature by the constitution, and any and every power not delegated to the other departments of the government, or other governmental agency, by the constitution, and properly assumed by the legislature, irrespective of its nature becomes legislative in the sense that it cannot be delegated to or exercised or controlled by any other department or authority.

By the general clause vesting judicial power in the courts, the constitutions do not vest in them all powers judicial in their nature, but only the power to determine and protect legal rights. The constitution certainly may vest other powers in the courts. The legislature also may delegate powers not specially delegated elsewhere by the constitution, and not already exercised by another department, to the courts. Any and every power vested by the constitution in the courts, or any and every power properly delegated to them by the legislature and exercised by them, irrespective of its nature, becomes judicial in the sense that it cannot be delgated to, exercised or controlled by, either of the other departments.

Besides vesting in the executive the power to see that the laws are faithfully executed, the constitutions vest in him many other powers, such as the veto power, and the power to remove for cause certain officers. The legislature also may delegate to the executive powers not vested by the

[1] See Kilbourn *vs.* Thompson.

constitution in either of the other departments, or other governmental authority. Any and every power, irrespective of its nature, vested in the executive by the constitution, or properly delegated to him by the legislature, and exercised by him, becomes executive in the sense that it cannot be delegated to, or exercised or controlled by, either of the other departments.

Any power not expressly vested by the constitution in either of the departments or other governmental authority, *irrespective of its nature*, may be assumed by the legislature, or delegated to either of the other departments or any other governmental agency without violating the distributing clause.

It is in regard to the last proposition that the greatest confusion has arisen. Every now and then the community is startled by the assumption by the legislature, or the delegation to the executive, of an administrative power, judicial in its nature. Every now and then the courts resent a delegation to them of administrative power, because not judicial in its nature, on the ground that it is a violation of the principle herein considered.

From the preceding proposition it becomes important exactly to determine what is meant by the legislative, the judicial, and especially by the executive department of government.

The departments of which the constitutions speak, and in respect to which they provide that no person employed in one shall be employed in either of the other two, and that no power exercised by the one shall be exercised or controlled by the others, are the departments of the commonwealth governments (as distinguished from those of local governments) as expressly organized, defined and limited in the constitutions; and the meaning of the provision is that no member of the legislative department as therein defined shall at the same time be a member of the judicial or the executive department as therein organized and defined, and vice versa. Therefore there is nothing in the article which prohibits a judicial officer from exercising functions not in their nature judicial, if they do not belong either to the legislative or the executive department as those departments are defined and limited in the constitution.[1]

The power of allotting to the different departments of government their appropriate functions is a legislative power, and in so far as the distribution is not made in the constitution, the power to make it is vested in the general assembly as the depositary of the legislative power of the commonwealth. It follows that in many cases power may appropriately be assigned to and exercised by either of the departments.[2] Thus, as will subsequently appear, the legislature may prescribe rules of practice for the courts, or may authorize the courts to make them. It may vest the power of removing officers for cause, whether such power be considered administrative or judicial, in the governor,[3] in the courts, or in inferior administrative bodies. The power to try contested elections may be vested in the courts or assumed by the legislature.[4] There are powers strictly legislative, others strictly executive, and others strictly judicial, while still others may be exercised by one department or by another, as the law may provide.

The constitutions do not define the extent or prescribe the limits of judicial power. The judicial power is, in our constitutions, whatever the laws of the commonwealth from time to

[1] People *vs.* Provines, 34 Cal. 520. This entire subject is more fully considered hereafter. It is submitted that much would be gained if we would apply the term administrative to all officers not belonging either to the executive, the legislative, or the judicial department, and to all powers not vested by the constitution in either of the departments. The following generalization would then result from the distributing clause: The legislature may assume or delegate to the executive or the courts, or even to a single administrative authority, all or any administrative powers, be they legislative, executive or judicial in their nature; and any administrative power properly exercised by the legislature, the courts or the executive becomes by force of the clause legislative, judicial or executive, and therefore would be beyond the control of any other authority.

[2] State *vs.* Harmon, 31 Ohio St. 250; Smith *vs.* Normant, 5 Yerg. 271.

[3] State *vs.* Peterson, 52 N. W. 655.

[4] State *vs.* Harmon, 31 Ohio St., 250.

time declare it to be. When any subject is declared by law to be of judicial cognizance, it becomes a part of the judicial power, in the only sense in which that term in the constitution can have any practical operation. Other departments of government, while it so remains a judicial power, are forbidden to exercise it. No subject, although in its nature judicial, can under our constitutions be regarded as coming within the judicial power, unless it has been assigned to the judicial department. Therefore a divorce is to be regarded as neither strictly a judicial nor a legislative act; and there is no reason why the granting of a divorce may not be either a legislative or a judicial act—legislative when it is performed as a mere exercise of sound discretion for the good of the parties and the public, and judicial when the divorce is demanded as a right under established law in consequence of some breach of duty committed by the offending party.[1]

Whenever a power is not distinctly either legislative, executive or judicial, and is not by the constitution confided to a designated department of the government, the mode of its exercise and the agency must necessarily be determined by law, in other words, must necessarily be under the control of the legislature.[2]

As already said, any power, whatever its nature, necessarily takes its character from the department to which it is assigned by the constitution or the legislature.

Whatever emanates from a judge as such, or proceeds from courts of justice, is judicial,[3] and whatever power or duty is imposed upon the executive department is executive, and therefore free from interference by the other branches of the government.[4] Certain powers may be exercised by either of the three departments or by any administrative authority; but,

[1] Op. of Justices, 16 Me. 479; Adams *vs.* Palmer, 51 Me. 480.

[2] Cooley's *Principles of Constitutional Law*, p. 44; Ross *vs.* Whitman, 6 Cal. 361.

[3] In re Cooper, 22 N. Y. 67. [4] Attorney-General *vs.* Brown, 1 Wis. 513.

when vested in the courts, they become judicial.[1] The power to try contested elections, when vested in the courts, is judicial; when it is not so vested, but is assumed by the legislature, it is legislative and may not be controlled by the courts.[2] The exercise of the power of eminent domain vested in county and township boards, and in corporations, is not the exercise of judicial power, within the meaning of the constitution, while the exercise of the same power by the courts, if vested in them, would be judicial.[3]

Attributing to the terms of the distributing clauses their properly restricted meaning, it follows that the legislature may delegate to administrative authorities administrative powers, judicial in their nature, of a very far-reaching character.

Whenever the legislature creates a new right, it may grant it, subject to any conditions which it sees fit to impose. Thus Congress, having full control over the right of aliens to enter or to remain in the United States, may make the right depend upon the decision of any authority, and may make the decision of such authority final and conclusive even upon the courts.[4]

Among the many powers of a far-reaching nature vested in officers not belonging to any of the departments of government, is that of administrative officers to impose penalties for the violation of law,[5] and even to arrest for such violation without resort to the courts,[6] as in the case of non-payment of taxes.[7]

[1] In re Cooper, 22 N. Y. 67.

[2] State *vs.* Harmon, 31 Ohio St. 250.

[3] *Ibid.* In re City of Buffalo, 139 N. Y. 422, indicates how far the court, in the exercise of the power of eminent domain, acts by virtue of power delegated to it by the Constitution, and how far by virtue of administrative power delegated to it by the legislature. See In re Hall, 5 Pa. St. 204.

[4] In re Howard, 63 Fed. Rep. 263; U. S. *vs.* Rogers, 65 Id. 787.

[5] Cooley on *Taxation*, p. 457; Parker and Worthington, *Public Health and Safety*, p. 103.

[6] Commonwealth *vs.* Byrne, 20 Gratt. 165–198.

[7] Cooley on *Taxation*, p. 437. For other examples of administrative execution without judicial process, see Goodnow's *Administrative Law*, vol. 2, p. 127.

Where the legislature vests important administrative powers in an administrative body or officer, the practice is now becoming popular of granting to individuals a right to appeal from the decision of such body or officer, to an administrative body or officer of a higher grade, and in some instances even to one of the departments.

Thus the United States patent law allows an appeal from the decision of an examiner rejecting an application for a patent to the examiner-in-chief; then from the decison of the examiner-in-chief, confirming the rejection, to the commissioner; and, in certain cases, from his decision, if adverse to the applicant, to the Supreme Court of the District of Columbia.[1]

The income tax law of August 29, 1894 (Sec. 29), authorized any person feeling aggrieved by the decision of a deputy collector as to the amount of income liable to be taxed, to appeal to the collector of the district, and from his decision to the commissioner of internal revenue.[2]

The customs administrative act of June 10, 1890, gives to the circuit courts of the United States power to reverse or *amend* the decisions, even of fact, of the Board of General Appraisers as to the classification for duty under the act.[3]

In the State of New York, if a person feels aggrieved by the decision of assessors as to the value of his property for purposes of taxation, courts may, on certiorari, reverse or *amend* the decision of the assessors on grounds of illegality, unfairness or disproportionality.[4]

Some judges have been at a loss to understand how the legislature may ultimately vest in the courts powers primarily vested in an administrative officer.

A statute passed by the legislature of New York in 1893,

[1] *U. S. Rev. St.*, secs. 4910–4912. See Butterworth *vs.* U. S., 112 U. S. 50; U. S. *vs.* Land Co., 148 U. S. 31.

[2] The decision declaring the law unconstitutional was not based on this provision.

[3] *U. S. Laws*, 1889–1890, chap. 407, sec. 15.

[4] *N. Y. Laws*, 1880, chap. 209.

provides that courts in certiorari proceedings *may command* a board of excise to grant a license to an applicant upon the payment of the proper license fee.[1]

The court, in construing this act, on one occasion declared that the legislature was without power to require courts or the judges thereof to perform other than judicial duties, and that it seemed that a provision of law which required courts to pass upon facts and reasons upon which a board of excise took action, apart from alleged errors of law, would be unconstitutional, as imposing upon the courts other than judicial functions.[2] On a subsequent occasion, the court said it seemed that the legislature could not assign to the courts, or to the justices thereof, the performance of administrative duties, such as are devolved upon boards of excise, boards of health, and boards of supervisors. It held that since the statute vested a discretion in the court, the court was not required to usurp a non-judicial function.[3]

In construing the distributing clause, the courts have formulated certain general definitions and rules of construction, which are more or less relied upon in their decisions.

It is said, " The difference between the departments undoubtedly is that the legislature makes, the executive executes, and the judiciary construes the laws."[4] It is the province of the legislature, "jus dare, non dicere;" of the judiciary, "jus dicere, non dare." " The distinction," says Justice Field in the Sinking Fund Cases, " between a judicial and legislative act is well defined. The one determines what the law is, and what the rights of the parties are with reference to transactions already had; the other provides what the law shall be in future cases arising

[1] *Laws*, 1893, chap. 481. The New York election laws likewise provide for a review by the supreme court, or any of its justices, of the acts and determinations of certain election officers. Laws of 1895, chap. 810, sec. 1, § 56.

[2] People *vs.* Waters, 4 Misc. Rep. 1.

[3] People *vs.* Dalton, 9 Misc. Rep. 249.

[4] Per. Ch. J. Marshall, Wayman *vs.* Southard, 10 Wheat. 46.

under it. Whenever an act undertakes to determine a question of right or obligation, or of property, as the foundation on which it proceeds, such act is to that extent a judicial one, and not the proper exercise of legislative functions."[1] It is the province of the judicial power to decide private disputes between or concerning persons, but of the legislative power to regulate public concerns and to make laws for the benefit and welfare of the state.[2] It is the province of the courts to decide what the law is or has been, and to determine its application to particular facts in the decision of cases; the province of the legislature to declare what the law shall be in the future.[3] The distinction lies between a sentence and a rule.[4] The legislature acts from considerations of public policy, the courts are guided by the pleadings and evidence in the case.[5]

"The legislative power we understand to be the authority under the constitution to make laws, and to alter and repeal them. Laws, in the sense in which the term is here employed, are rules of civil conduct which the legislative will prescribes."[6]

Judge Story says: "The laws of a state are usually understood to mean the rules and enactments promulgated by the legislative authority thereof."[7]

Each of the three departments has all there is of the element assigned it. Each department has, it is true, incidental rights of a nature *intrinsically different from the body of the power distributed to it*, but these incidental rights are such only as are necessary to enable it to perform its functions *as an independent branch* of the government, and are in fact part of the

[1] 99 U. S. 168. [2] Merril *vs.* Sherburne, 1 N. H. 199.

[3] Ratcliffe *vs.* Anderson, 30 Grat. 107. [4] *Ex parte* Shrader, 33 Cal. 279.

[5] Taylor *vs.* Place, 4 R. I. 324. "The judicial power mentioned in the Constitution and vested in the courts means the power conferred upon the courts in the strict sense of that term, courts that compose one of the three great departments of government, and *not power judicial in nature* or *quasi-judicial*, sometimes invested in individuals for particular purposes or limited times." Mr. Justice Wilson's Charge to the Grand Jury on the Fugitive Slave Law, 1 Blatchf. 635.

[6] Cooley's *Const. Limitations*, p. 108. [7] Swift *vs.* Tyson, 16 Pet. 18.

principal power itself.[1] How far the power of giving the law may involve every other power in cases where the constitution is silent, never has been, and perhaps never can be, definitely settled.[2]

It will hereafter appear that the authorities are in irreconcilable conflict as to whether the content of the departments should be determined by historical tests. However, as illustrative of the historical interpretation, it has been said that "what constitutes judicial power within the meaning of the constitution is to be determined in the light of the common law and of the history of our institutions as they existed anterior to and at the time of the adoption of the constitution."[3] And again, "When the constitutions vested in certain courts judicial power, they vested in such courts such powers as courts under the English and American systems had always exercised in that class of actions.[4]

It will be the humble endeavor of the succeeding pages to indicate how far the distributing clause, irrespective of other constitutional provisions, has affected the decisions of the courts.

[1] State *vs.* Noble, 118 Ind. 350.

[2] Fletcher *vs.* Peck, 6 Cranch, 87, 136.

[3] State *vs.* Harmon, 31 Ohio, 250.

[4] Cullman *vs.* Judd, 23 Wis. 343, 349.

PART III

THE LEGISLATURE AND THE COURTS

CHAPTER IX

DECLARATORY STATUTES OR LEGISLATIVE INTERPRETATION

Although, without one dissentient opinion, it is admitted that it is the exclusive province of the judiciary ultimately to construe and interpret the constitution and laws when called upon to do so in the course of a judicial controversy, the legislatures often seek to assume this power by the enactment of declaratory or expository laws. Bouvier defines a declaratory statute as one which is passed to put an end to a doubt as to what is the common law, or the meaning of another statute, and which declares what it is and ever has been.[1] Such a statute always is in a certain sense retrospective; and it is specially important where doubts have already arisen, as it may be found to declare the law to be different from what the courts have already adjudged it to be. The legislature attempts to put its own construction upon the law rather than the construction of the court, and in effect declares the judicial interpretation to be unfounded and unwarrantable.

If such a law is to have its intended effect, it must be considered by the courts either as creating a new rule for the government of past cases, or as declaring the interpretation of

[1] *Law Dictionary*, Statute.

former statutes for the direction of the courts. The act should not be construed to operate in either manner.

Under either alternative, such an act is open to every objection which can be urged against retrospective laws, other than *curative* laws.

It is a principle of the English common law, as ancient as the law itself, that a statute even of its omnipotent parliament should not be construed to have retroactive effect. This maxim of the common law as laid down by Bracton and Coke was probably taken from the civil law.[1] It was also recognized as a fundamental truth by the French Code.[2] New Hampshire, Texas, Ohio, Louisiana, Missouri, Colorado, and Tennessee have deemed it advisable to forbid retroactive laws by their constitutions.

Nevertheless, retrospective laws, provided they do not contravene express constitutional limitations, especially those forbidding the impairment of vested rights by the legislature, are within the legislative competency.[3]

There being no vested right in a particular remedy, the legislature may change remedies, alter rules of evidence,[4] and vary the periods of prescription and limitation, and make the laws as modified apply to transactions already past.

On the ground that the legislature has full power to change remedies, statutes closing courts, and suspending the operation of civil process or the rendition of judgments for a reasonable

[1] *Dig.* 50, 17, 75; *Code* 1, 14, 7.

[2] *Code de Civil des Français*, no. 2.

[3] There is nothing in the Constitution of the United States to prohibit the several commonwealths from passing retroactive laws, even if they divest rights vested by law in individuals, so long as they do not impair the obligation of contracts or partake of the nature of ex post facto laws or bills of attainder. Satterlee *vs.* Mathewson, 2 Pet. 413; Watson *vs.* Mercer, 8 Pet. 85; Freeland *vs.* Williams, 131 U. S. 405. See Sturges *vs.* Carter, 114 U. S. 511. A legislature may always constitutionally pass a retroactive law impairing its own rights. See Mayers *vs.* Byrne, 19 Ark. 308.

[4] Cooley, *Const. Limitations*, p. 450.

time, are not unconstitutional. They do not affect the remedy so injuriously as to render the right worthless.[1]

So, likewise, it is held that the repeal of a limitation of actions on personal debts, does not, as applied to a debtor against whom the right of action is already barred, unduly deprive him of property.[2]

The retroactive statutes with which we are most concerned, are those curing defects in legal proceedings. Commenting upon these, Judge Cooley observes:[3] "Such statutes, if they are only in aid of judicial proceedings, and tend to their support by precluding parties from taking advantage of errors which do not affect substantial rights, cannot be obnoxious to the charge of usurping judicial power. The legislature does, or may, prescribe the rules under which the judicial power is exercised by the courts, and in so doing it may dispense with any of those formalities which are not essential to the jurisdiction of the court; and whatever it may dispense with by statute anterior to the proceedings, it is believed it may also dispense with by statute after the proceedings have been taken, if the court has failed to observe any of those formalities."[4]

Of such nature are statutes validating the sale of lands erroneously described in a petition for sale,[5] and statutes providing that no levy of execution on real estate previously made shall be deemed void, because the officer embraced in the return thereof, as part of the costs of the levy, greater and other fees than were by law allowable.[6]

But a curative act of the legislature undertaking to confirm judicial proceedings absolutely void, for want of jurisdiction or other cause, would be an attempted exercise of judicial power, and an unwarrantable encroachment by the legislature on

[1] Coxe *vs.* Martin, 44 Pa. St. 322; Breitenbach *vs.* Bush, 44 Pa. St. 313.

[2] Campbell *vs.* Holt, 115 U. S. 620.

[3] *Const. Limitations*, p. 126.

[4] See also Cooley's *Const. Limitations*, p. 454; Black on *Constitutional Prohibitions*, sec. 210.

[5] Lane *vs.* Nelson, 79 Pa. St. 407.

[6] Booth *vs.* Booth, 7 Conn. 350.

the judicial department. If the proceedings are void, it would be the statute alone which would in such case constitute an adjudication upon the rights of the parties. So where by reason of non-compliance with the law regulating constructive service, jurisdiction has not attached, a retroactive statute cannot cure the defect.[1]

Even in those commonwealths where retrospective laws are specifically prohibited by the constitutions, there are certain classes of statutes of that character which are considered valid and constitutional as being salutary and wholesome regulations, and not within the just construction of the inhibition.[2] Such laws are often necessary for the enforcement of justice, as when a mere irregularity would otherwise make a good transaction void. It is generally recognized that a statute expressly retroactive, the object of which is to correct an innocent mistake, to remedy a mischief, to execute the intentions of parties and to promote justice, as a matter of right and public policy should be sustained. Such a statute does not deprive a party of a vested right, because a party cannot have a vested right to do a wrong.[3]

Although retrospective curative acts may in some cases be unobjectionable, retrospective expository acts declaring how former statutes are to be interpreted or construed in their application to transactions already past, are in every case objectionable and unconstitutional. If such interpretation or construction by the legislature is to be considered as giving the former acts a new meaning, it then becomes a new rule, and is to have the same effect as any other newly created statute. But if it is to be considered as an exposition of the former acts for the information and government of the courts in the decision of causes before them, the legislature would

[1] Israel *vs.* Arthur, 7 Col. 5; Pryer *vs.* Downey, 50 Cal. 388; Daniell *vs.* Correll, 19 Ill. 226.

[2] See Dimson *vs.* Bank, 36 N. H. 466; Raixden *vs.* Holden, 15 Ohio St. 207.

[3] Cooley's *Const. Limitations*, pp. 460-477.

then be taking cognizance of a judicial question.[1] Should the legislature by statute declare what was the intention of a former act, or prescribe that a former act should or should not be construed in a certain manner, and provide that such declaratory law should have retroactive as well as prospective force, the courts must declare it void as an assumption of judicial power by the legislature. Should a declaratory statute have the intended retroactive effect, it would amount to a legislative mandate to the court, establishing a particular interpretation upon a particular statute, thus exercising a judicial power in settling a question of interpretation, and subordinating the judiciary as a co-ordinate department.[2] Accordingly, it has been held that a mandate of the legislature to the judiciary directing what construction shall be placed on an existing statute is unconstitutional.[3] Had the legislature power to give to declaratory acts their intended effect, it would in every case in which it felt so disposed, sit as a court of review to which parties might appeal when dissatisfied with the rulings of the court.[4] The acts of the legislature are committed to writing, and it is by the written language that their sense is to be ascertained, and not by a subsequent legislative body which differs in organization from the body which enacted the law. Such arbitrary interpretation of a law would not be a legal interpretation, but a substitution of the language and meaning of one legislative body for the other. Therefore where the courts held that insurance companies were taxable to a certain extent under an existing statute, a subsequent act of the legislature declaring that it was intended that they should be taxable at a certain other rate, and that such was the true intention and construction of the original statute, was held void as far as it was in-

[1] Dash *vs.* Van Kleeck, 7 Johns. 477.

[2] People *vs.* Board of Supervisors, 16 N. Y. 424; Greenough *vs.* Greenough, 11 Pa. St. 489.

[3] Governor *vs.* Porter, 5 Humph. 165.

[4] Greenough *vs.* Greenough, *supra.*

tended to have retroactive force.[1] So where the courts construed a law, declaring that every incorporated company must annually within twenty days of the first of January publish a report, to mean whenever January came after the organization of the corporation, a subsequent act declaring the word annually as used in the prior act to have meant once a year after such corporation had been doing business at least twelve months, was held void so far as it was retroactive.[2]

It is evident that the legislature has no authority to interpret or define words of the constitution for the courts,[3] or to declare a matter of constitutional construction, nor can it set aside a construction of a constitutional provision which has become fixed and settled by judicial determination. So where the constitution of Georgia entitled the head of a family to enter a homestead, and the courts decided that a single person having no others dependent upon him could not be regarded as the head of a family though keeping house with servants, an act declaring any single person living habitually as housekeeper to himself should be regarded as the head of a family, was held void.[4] And where the courts had construed the meaning of "former jeopardy" as used in the constitution, an act of the legislature making it mean no more than legal conviction, was held unconstitutional.[5]

Similarly, the legislative branch of the government cannot, by a statutory enactment, declare an act of its own to be either constitutional or void, though it may repeal, or refuse to enact, any law because it deems it unconstitutional, irrespective of whether or not the courts declare it constitutional.[6] The con-

1 People *vs.* Board of Supervisors, 16 N. Y. 424.

2 Union Iron Co. *vs.* Pierce, 4 Bissel, 327.

3 Westinghausen *vs.* People, 44 Mich. 263; comp. People *vs.* Supervisors of La Salle, 100 Ill. 495.

4 Calhoun *vs.* McLendon, 42 Ga. 405.

5 Powell *vs.* The State, 17 Texas Appeal, 345.

6 See In re Lafayette Co., 2 Chaud. (Wis.) 212; In re Ruan Street, 132 Pa. St. 257, 279.

struction of a statute being a judicial power, the attempt of the legislature to exercise such power by adding a proviso to a law that "nothing herein contained shall be construed as authorizing a lottery in this State, or as allowing the sale of lottery tickets, contrary to the provisions of the constitution," is an unconstitutional assumption of the functions of the judiciary.[1]

Until the judiciary has fixed the meaning of a doubtful law upon which rights have become vested, it may be explained by legislative enactment; and, when explanatory statutes are designed to explain doubtful statutes, they deserve the attention of the judiciary.[2] But when the words and intent of the act are so explicit and plain that no court has ever been appealed to, to declare their meaning, the legislature cannot by a retroactive law put a construction upon them contrary to their obvious letter and spirit.[3]

Since courts will give effect to laws if they possibly can, and since the legislature can make laws looking to the future, declaratory statutes will be held to govern cases arising after the statute was passed.[4] If a statute should combine retrospective and prospective criminal legislation, in so far as the two are separable the latter part will be held good.[5]

But some courts refuse to apply this rule of construction, and intimate that if the legislature would prescribe a different rule for the future from that which the courts enforce, it must be done by a new law, and cannot be done by a mandate to the courts which leaves the law unchanged, but seeks to compel the courts to construe and apply it not according to judicial

[1] *Ex parte* Blanchard, 9 Mo. 101.

[2] O'Conner *vs.* Warren, 4 W. & S. 223; Gough *vs.* Pratt, 9 Md. 526; Lamberton *vs.* Hogan, 2 Pa. St. 22.

[3] Reiser *vs.* Wm. Tell Association, 39 Pa. St. 137.

[4] Greenough *vs.* Greenough, 11 Pa. St. 489.

[5] Jackson *vs.* People, 128 U. S. 189.

but according to legislative judgment.[1] The legislature cannot compel courts for the future to adopt a particular construction of a law which the legislature permits to remain in force.

Finally, under the constitution of Pennsylvania,[2] which provides that no law shall be revived, amended, or extended by a reference to its title only, but that so much thereof as is revived, amended, or extended, shall be reënacted and published at length, the courts deem themselves prohibited from giving effect, even as to future cases, to expository or declaratory acts.[3]

[1] Governor *vs.* Porter, 5 Humph. 165.

[2] Art. 3, Sec. 6.

[3] Titusville Iron Works *vs.* Keystone Oil Co., 122 Pa. St. 627.

CHAPTER X

LEGISLATIVE ASSUMPTION OF JUDICIAL POWERS

ALTHOUGH glaringly in conflict with the constitutional clause under consideration, legislatures have not infrequently enacted laws which, if given the effect intended, would result in legislative judgments. It has been held that the foreclosure of a mortgage on private property cannot be accomplished by a legislative enactment.[1] The legislature has no power to inquire, ascertain, or determine whether a widow is entitled to dower in a specified parcel of land, and an act authorizing commissioners to assign to her her dower in certain premises is void, as far as it is a determination that she is entitled to dower therein, it being a judicial determination.[2]

Likewise it has been held that whether a corporation has been guilty of an abuse of its corporate privileges so as justly to subject it to a forfeiture, is a question to be decided by the courts and not by the legislature.[3] For this reason among others it is held that the charter of a bank cannot be declared forfeited by a proclamation of the governor made under an act of the legislature. And the act itself authorizing the executive, upon sufficient proof being made to him of the existence of facts, to make the forfeiture known by his proclamation, is void. The dissolving of a corporation or declaring a forfeiture of its charter is the province of the bench, the exercise of judicial power.[4] The forfeiture of a corporate charter

[1] Ashuelot R. R. Co. *vs.* Elliot, 58 N. H. 451.

[2] Edwards *vs.* Pope, 4 Ill. 465.

[3] State *vs.* Noyes, 47 Me. 189.

[4] Campbell *vs.* Mississippi Union Bk., 6 How. (Miss.) 625.

can be enforced only by judicial proceedings instituted for that purpose at the instance of the government.[1]

But a reservation by the legislature of the right to repeal an act of incorporation for a violation of its provisions or other default, is not unconstitutional. The exercise of a reserved power of amending and repealing the charter of a corporation is a legislative power.[2] Nor is the inquiry by the legislature into the affairs or defaults of a corporation with a view to continue or discontinue it, a judicial act.[3] A clause in a charter authorizing the legislature to repeal it for an "abuse or misuse of corporate privileges" refers the question of abuse to legislative judgment.[4]

Where the legislature reserves in the charter a right to repeal it for abuse or misuse of corporate powers, a repealing act is constitutional unless the corporation can show by plain and satisfactory evidence that the privileges granted were not abused or misused.[5]

But it has also been held in some jurisdictions that, where a charter contains a provision that it shall not be repealed "unless it shall be made to appear to the legislature that there has been a violation by the corporation of some of the provisions of the charter," the question of violation nevertheless is a judicial question, and that the charter cannot be repealed until the violation has been made to appear to the legislature by some proper judicial proceeding before a judicial tribunal. An act simply providing "the charter is hereby repealed" was held void as the exercise by the legislature of judicial power.[6]

[1] Canal Co. *vs.* Railroad Co., 4 G. & J. 1.

[2] Ashuelot R. R. Co. *vs.* Elliot, 58 N. H. 451.

[3] Lothrop *vs.* Stedman, 42 Conn. 583; Crease *vs.* Babcock, 23 Pick. 334; Allen *vs.* Buchanan, 9 Phil. (Pa.) 283; Regents *vs.* Williams, 9 G. & J. 365.

[4] Miners' Bk. *vs.* United States, 1 Morris, 482.

[5] Erie & Northeast R. R. Co. *vs.* Casey, 26 Pa. St. 287; Commonwealth *vs.* Pittsburgh R. R. Co., 58 Pa. St. 46. See Mowrawetz on *Private Corp.*, Sec. 112.

[6] Flint & Fentonville R. R. Co. *vs.* Woodhull, 25 Mich. 99.

Although where the right to repeal or amend a charter depends upon some contingency, some act or omission of the corporation, the right to judge whether that contingency has occurred belongs generally to the legislature, not to the courts,[1] yet the power of the legislature is limited to the destruction of the powers it gave to the corporation, as part of its existence, and does not extend to the destruction of the property rights which it acquired through the exercise of such powers.[2]

Upon the ground that the legislature may exercise administrative powers, legislative appointments of trustees to sell property of persons *non sui juris* are maintained.[3] Upon the ground that the legislature may delegate to any officer or body, whether created by the constitution or by itself, or to any department of the government, administrative powers, or powers not specifically vested by the constitution in any one of the departments or in any other officer or body, an act authorizing the governor to appoint a receiver to settle the affairs of an insolvent bank, is constitutional, and an appointment thereunder, valid.[4]

The legislature was also sustained in the appointment of a trustee to take the assets and manage the affairs of a corporation whose charter had been repealed. The court said: "If no trustee were appointed by the legislature, a court of equity, which never allows a trust to fail for want of a trustee, would see to the execution of the trust."[5]

For the legislature to assume in any manner directly or indirectly to control the courts in the decision of causes or in the rendering of final judgments, as by revising or annulling their judgments or interfering with the adjudications they

[1] McLaren *vs.* Pennington, 1 Paige (N. Y.) 102.

[2] People *vs.* O'Brien, 45 Hun. 519.

[3] Hindman *vs.* Piper, 50 Mo. 292; Rice *vs.* Parkham, 16 Mass. 326; Cochran *vs.* Van Surlay, 20 Wend. 373.

[4] Carey *vs.* Giles, 9 Ga. 253.

[5] Lothrop *vs.* Stedman, 42 Conn. 583.

have duly and formally reached, would be the assumption of judicial power, and therefore contrary to the principle of the separation of powers.

It has been shown that the legislature cannot compel the courts to apply a legislative interpretation of a law.[1] It follows from the same principles that the legislature has no power of directing what particular steps shall be taken in the progress of a judicial inquiry. Therefore an act directing that certain depositions which had previously been taken should be read in evidence on a trial, notwithstanding certain informalities, is void.[2] Nor can the legislature prescribe for the courts what instructions they shall give in a particular pending cause, unless they have previously embodied in a legislative enactment, as the law of the land, the substance of such instructions.[3]

No act of the legislature can alter the nature or legal effect of an existing contract, or give to such contract a judicial construction which shall be binding upon the parties or upon the courts.[4]

Since the legislature has no judicial power, the preamble of a private statute cannot be used by the courts as evidence of matters recited therein. The legislature has no power to find facts by legislative enactment so as to be evidence in suits pending before the courts.[5]

Although the case or controversy might have been such in its nature that the legislature could have acted upon it, had it seen fit, without the aid of the courts, and without encroaching upon the just claims of the judicial department, yet if a suit should be brought upon it and be pending in the courts, the legislature could not control its subsequent progress. Any

[1] Taylor *vs.* Place, 4 R. I. 324.

[2] Dufy *vs.* Wickwire, 1 D. Chip. 238; s. c., 6 Am. Dec. 729.

[3] State *vs.* Hopper, 71 Mo. 425.

[4] King *vs.* Bank, 15 Mass. 447; Weaver *vs.* Maillot, 15 La. Ann. 395.

[5] Elmendorf *vs.* Carmechal, 3 Litt. 475. See Lothrop *vs.* Stedman, 42 Conn. 583, 592.

attempt on the part of the legislature to exercise its power over the court or the decision of the suit would be the exercise ot judicial power. Thus Congress may collect, by means of administrative officers of the United States, balances due to the United States from receivers of public money without the aid of the courts. But as it is competent for the government to sue any of its depositors in a court of law, or consent to itself being sued, if such a suit be brought and pending in a court of the United States, it would be so completely within judicial control that Congress could not by subsequent action control its progress or decision.[1]

If anything is self-evident in the structure of our government, it is that the legislature has no power to order a rehearing or new trial, or to direct the court to order them, either before or after judgment. Such power is judicial.[2] An act of the legislature, however, granting a new trial or reopening a judment in favor of the people, is a mere consent on the part of the people, one of the parties to the judgment, that a new trial be granted or judgment reopened, and is not unconstitutional.[3]

Nor has the legislature power to grant to parties a right to appeal after it is gone under the general law.[4] But a statute which takes away the right to a future appeal in an action already pending, but undetermined, when the statute takes effect, is not unconstitutional.[5] After the time prescribed by law for asking a new trial or taking an appeal has expired, the judgment becomes final between the parties, and no subsequent

[1] Murray's Lessee *vs.* Hoboken Land and Improvement Co., 18 Howard, 272, 283.

[2] De Chastellux *vs.* Fairchild, 15 Pa. St. 18; Durham *vs.* Lewiston, 4 Me. 140; Griffin's Executors *vs.* Cunningham, 20 Gratt. 31. See Lawson *vs.* Jeffries, 47 Miss. 686, which held that the constitutional convention of Mississippi of 1888, being a legislative body, had no power to grant new trials, such power being judicial.

[3] People *vs.* Frisbie, 26 Cal. 135.

[4] Hill *vs.* Sunderland, 3 Vt. 507; Lewis *vs.* Webb, 3 Me. 326.

[5] Grover *vs.* Coon, 1 N. Y. 536; *ex parte* McCardle, 7 Wall. (U. S.) 506; R. R. Co. *vs.* Grant, 98 U. S. 398.

legislature can confer the right to a new trial or an appeal in such action.[1] But there are some cases which hold that the legislature has power to confer on the courts the right to hear appeals in special cases[2], even after the time allowed by the general laws for an appeal has passed.[3]

In order to preserve the independence of the judiciary as a co-ordinate branch of the government, final judgments of the courts must be beyond the influence and power of the legislature.

In some jurisdictions it has been held that an act providing for graduated deductions from the sentence of imprisonment, as a reward for good conduct, is unconstitutional, because an interference with the judgment of the court sentencing the criminal.[4]

An act reversing and annulling a judgment is unconstitutional.[5] So an act of the legislature opening judgments is the exercise of judicial power, and therefore void.[6] It cannot reopen or set aside a final judgment nor compel the courts to do so, no matter how erroneous the judgment may be.[7] A judgment of the court becomes final when by the existing laws the time for a review and reversal for error has expired.[8]

A legislative act directing the levy and collection of a tax which has already been declared illegal by the judiciary, is inoperative and void, as an attempted reversal of judicial action by the legislature.[9]

[1] Sydnor *vs.* Palmer, 32 Wis. 406.

[2] State *vs.* Northern R. R. Co., 18 Md. 193.

[3] Page *vs.* Administrator, 40 Ala. 547; Prout *vs.* Berry, 2 Gill, 147.

[4] Commonwealth *vs.* Halloway, 42 Pa. St. 446. See State *vs.* Fleming, 7 Humph. 152.

[5] Opinion of the judges in the matter of Dorr, 3 R. I. 299.

[6] Taylor *vs.* Place, 4 R. I. 324.

[7] Ratcliffe *vs.* Anderson, 31 Gratt. 105; Arnold *vs.* Kelly, 5 W. Va. 446.

[8] Atkinson *vs.* Dunlap, 50 Me. 111.

[9] Mayor *vs.* Horn, 26 Md. 194; Butler *vs.* Supervisors of Saginaw, 26 Mich. 22. See Forster *vs.* Forster, 129 Mass. 559.

Nor can the legislature by a law practically dissolve an injunction of a court.[1] An act prescribing that no injunction shall be issued against commissioners of certain public works, has been declared invalid.[2] But the constitutionality of acts providing that "no suits for the purpose of restraining the assessment or collection of any tax,"[3] shall be maintained in any court, has been frequently reasserted—provided only that the statute leaves to the person, who considers himself aggrieved by the collection of the tax, the usual remedy of an action at law to recover back the amount paid.[4]

It is universally conceded that the legislature may prescribe and change rules of procedure for the courts.[5] The legislature in undertaking to regulate the rules of pleading does not usurp judicial functions.[6] It may prescribe such rules for the trial and determination as well of existing as of future rights and controversies as in its judgment will most completely subserve the ends of justice.[7]

The rules of evidence are at all times subject to the modification and control of the legislature, the only implied limitation upon the power of the legislature in such case being that it cannot by the exercise of its power deprive a party of the right to a fair trial. It has power to prescribe what shall be

[1] Scarcy *vs.* Turnpike Co., 79 Ind. 274.

[2] Guy *vs.* Hermance, 5 Cal. 73.

[3] U. S. Rev. St., Sec. 3224.

[4] Moore *vs.* Com'rs of Internal Revenue, Sup. Ct., Dist. of Columbia, Jan'y, 1895; Snyder *vs.* Marks, 109 U. S. 192, and cases cited. See Antoni *vs.* Greenhow, 107 U. S. 769, upholding the validity of a statute that denied to the courts the authority to issue writs of mandamus in litigation concerning coupons of commonwealth bonds, because the holders thereof still had other methods of asserting their rights.

[5] Matter of Stillwell, 139 N. Y. 337; *Ex parte* Hickey, 52 Ala. 228.

[6] Whiting *vs.* Townsend, 57 Cal. 515.

[7] Ogden *vs.* Saunders, 12 Wheat. 213; Delaplaine *vs.* Cook, 7 Wis. 44; Himmelman *vs.* Carpentier, 47 Cal. 42.

received as *prima facie* or presumptive evidence.[1] Even in criminal matters the legislature may enact that when certain facts have been proved, they shall be *prima facie* evidence of the main fact in question, provided they have some fair relation to or natural connection with such fact.[2] It has also been said that it may make that which, according to the ordinary rules of human experience, reasonably tends to prove a fact, conclusive evidence thereof.[3]

A question has been raised as to the extent of the authority of the legislature over the power of the courts to punish for contempt.

In California it has been said, " No authority denies the inherent right of a court in the absence of a limitation placed upon it by the power which created it, to punish as a contempt, an act, whether committed in or out of its presence, which tends to impede, embarass, or obstruct the court in the discharge of its duties. It is founded upon the principle (which is coeval with the existence of the courts, and as necessary as the right of self-protection) that it is a necessary incident to the execution of the powers conferred upon the court, and is necessary to maintain its dignity, if not its very existence. It exists independently of statutes. The legislative department may regulate its procedure, and enlarge the power, but it cannot without trenching upon the constitutional powers of the court, and destroying the autonomy of that system of checks and balances, which is one of the chief features of our triple-department form of government, fetter the power itself."[4]

In Arkansas the legislature sanctioned the power of the

[1] B'd of Com'rs *vs.* Merchant, 103 N. Y. 143; Law Encycl., vol. 3, p. 716; Hand *vs.* Ballou, 12 N. Y. 54; Howard *vs.* Moot, 64 N. Y. 262. See State *vs.* Cunningham, 25 Conn. 195; Gibbs *vs.* Gale, 7 Md. 76.

[2] People *vs.* Cannon, 139 N. Y. 32. See Cooley, *Const. Limitations*, p. 450.

[3] In re Linn County, 15 Kan. 500; People *vs.* Hill, 44 Hun. 472; Comp. Wantlan *vs.* White, 19 Ind. 470; Little Rock R. R. Co. *vs.* Payne, 33 Ark. 816.

[4] In re Shortridge, 34 Pac. R. 227.

court to punish as contempts certain enumerated acts and "*no others*."

The court declared that the sanction was merely declaratory of the common law, and that the prohibitory clause was not binding upon the courts. It declared that the legislature might regulate the exercise of but could not abridge the express or necessarily implied powers granted to the courts by the constitution, and that when the court was created and certain judicial powers were conferred upon it, the power to punish contempts of its authority was impliedly given to it as a necessary incident of the exercise of its express powers.[1]

In Colorado it has been held that the power of the courts to punish for contempt is not limited to cases expressly authorized by the legislature.[2] In New York, however, it has been admitted that the legislature has authority to limit the power of the courts in this regard, the court of appeals assuming, without discussion of the question, that such authority existed.[3]

In Georgia and Lousiana the constitutions expressly provide that the power shall be limited by the legislature, and in Arkansas, that the legislature shall have power to regulate by law the punishment of contempts not committed in the presence or hearing of the courts, or in disobedience of their process.[4]

[1] State *vs.* Morrill, 16 Ark. 384.

[2] People *vs.* Stapleton, 33 Pac. R. 167.

[3] People *vs.* Ct. of Oyer and Terminer, 101 N. Y. 243.

[4] Stimson's *Am. Statute Law*, Sec. 582.

CHAPTER XI

SPECIAL LAWS AUTHORIZING THE SALE OF LANDS

MANY of the acts before referred to, in addition to their constitutional invalidity, will also be found to be objectionable in their character of special laws. The legislatures having plenary powers in legislation, except as restricted by the constitutions, have the power of passing special or private laws. The number of persons upon whom any law is to operate does not affect its character and is immaterial.[1] Such special laws, even when not expressly prohibited by the constitutions, and not interfering with vested rights, are regarded with great jealousy, and rightly so, because "when in the exercise of proper legislative powers general laws are enacted which bear or may bear on the whole community, if they are unjust and against the spirit of the constitution, the whole community will be interested to procure their repeal by a voice potential. That is the great security for just and fair legislation. But when individuals are selected from the mass, and laws are enacted affecting their property without summons or notice, at the instigation of an interested party, who is to stand up for them, thus isolated from the mass in injury and injustice, or where are they to seek relief from such acts of despotic power?"[2] An idea of how extensively the legislatures have abused the power of enacting special laws may best be formed from the numerous provisions found in the constitution of every commonwealth, prohibiting special legislation in certain specified cases.

Our statute books are full of special laws empowering guar-

[1] Watkins *vs.* Holman, 16 Pet. 25.

[2] Ervine's Appeal, 16 Pa. St. 256, 268.

dians, and other persons in trust relations, to sell the lands of minors, of persons *non compotes mentis*, and of others resting under legal disabilities. The acts here described have under certain circumstances and for various reasons been quite universally recognized as a proper subject of legislative power. It has been held that there is nothing in its nature judicial in the granting permission, upon the application of a trustee, to convert by sale the real property of a *cestui que trust* into personal property, in order to effectuate the purpose of the trust, and to accomplish objects in the interest of the *cestui que trust*, not otherwise attainable. Such an act merely enlarges the sphere of the fiduciary authority, the better to accomplish the purposes for which the trusteeship was created. In such a proceeding there is no controversy between party and party, nor any decree or judgment affecting the title to property. The authority granted by the legislature to transmute real into personal property is exercised for purposes beneficial to all interested therein.

Moreover it is always taken into consideration that such power has been frequently exercised by the legislatures of the commonwealths, provinces and colonies. The constant exercise of a power by a legislature from the adoption of the constitution to the present time, it has been said, ought to be deemed almost conclusive evidence of its rightful possession by that body.

Furthermore, if it were not true that the legislature possesses the power in question, even general laws delegating to the courts the power to order the sale of lands, under which many estates of minors, of persons *non compotes mentis*, and of others, have been sold, would, together with the sales made under them, be void. For the courts, acting under those general laws, derived their authority from the legislatures; and the power not being of a judicial nature, if the legislatures had it not, they could not communicate it to any other body.[1] Accordingly it has been held that a private act

[1] Rice *vs.* Parkman, 16 Mass. 326; Clark *vs.* Van Surlay, 15 Wendell, 436.

of the legislature authorizing the sale of the estates of infants for their maintenance and education is within the scope of legislative authority. This power, it is said, is based on reason. It is the legitimate exercise of paternal power over the person and property of infants.[1] The Supreme Court of the United States has confirmed the constitutionality of a special act passed by a commonwealth legislature authorizing a court to decree, on the petition of an administrator, a private sale of the real estate of an intestate to pay his debts, even though the act did not require notice to the heirs or to any other person, and although the same subject was regulated by a general statute more provident in its nature. Such legislation was said to be remedial and not judicial. It infringed no contract and involved no usurpation of judicial power.[2] Such legislation determines no rights. It deprives no one of his property. It is a grant of a privilege to one person, which at the same time does not affect injuriously the rights of others. The Court of Appeals of New York has held that the legislature has power by special statute to authorize the sale of lands of infants, and that this power even extends to future contingent interests of those not in being.[3] The Supreme Court of the United States ruled that where an executor, who proved a will in New Hampshire, made an unauthorized sale of lands in Rhode Island, to satisfy the debts against his decedent's estate, a subsequent act of the Rhode Island legislature confirming the sale, was not an encroachment upon the judiciary. The lands descended to the heirs subject to a lien for the payment of such debts, and there is nothing in an act, authorizing the sale of lands to satisfy a lien, which requires that it should be done by a judicial tribunal, or that it should be performed by a delegate rather than by the legislature itself.[4]

[1] Cochran *vs.* Van Surlay, 20 Wendell, 365.

[2] Florentine *vs.* Barton, 2 Wallace, 210. See also Hoyt *vs.* Sprague, 103 U. S. 613.

[3] Brevoort *vs.* Grace, 53 N. Y. 245.

[4] Wilkinson *vs.* Leland, 2 Peters, 627; Acc'd Watkin's *vs.* Holman's Lessee, 16 Peters, 25.

It has been held that the legislature can grant this power of sale even to the very person under legal disability and for whose benefit it is to be made.[1]

Such a power, however, is legislative only so far as it is remedial. Accordingly, the legislature cannot against the will or without the consent of a person *sui juris*, seized of a vested right, authorize the sale of real estate.[2] It has no power to authorize, without their consent, the sale of lands in which adults competent to act for themselves have an interest vested or contingent.[3] A statute authorizing the sale of real estate on the petition of the life tenant in opposition to the wishes of the owner in fee when the latter is under no legal disability is unconstitutional.[4] Where a minor had a guardian, it was held incompetent for the legislature to empower another to sell his land.[5]

But, in any case, the ascertainment of indebtedness between two parties and the application of the property of one to the payment of the other, is a judicial act, and cannot be exercised by the legislature. So the legislature cannot pass an act authorizing the sale of so much of the decedent's land as would raise a specified sum, and order the proceeds to be applied to the extinguishment of certain claims against the deceased.[6] Nor has the legislature power to assume that debts are due and payable, and on that assumption to authorize an administrator to sell lands vested in heirs and apply the proceeds to the payment of the debts of the estate, without a judicial inquiry as to the existence of such debts before paying them.[7]

On the other hand, in some jurisdictions a different view is entertained. In Tennessee it is held that special acts authorizing

[1] McComb *vs.* Gilkey, 29 Miss. 146. [2] Hegarty's Appeal, 75 Pa. St. 503.

[3] Breevort *vs.* Grace, 53 N. Y. 245.

[4] Gossom *vs.* McFerran, 79 Ky. 236. See Linsby *vs.* Hubbard, 44 Conn. 109.

[5] Lincoln *vs.* Alexander 52 Cal. 482. [6] Lane *vs.* Doman, 4 Ill. 238.

[7] Rozier *vs.* Fagan, 46 Ill. 404. See Estep *vs.* Hutchman, 14 S. & R. 435.

guardians of the minor heirs of a deceased person to sell lands descended to the heirs, and the proceeds of the sale to be applied to the payment of debts created by the deceased during his lifetime, are unconstitutional because judicial in their nature.[1] In New Hampshire the validity of such special statutes is also denied.[2] It is there said that the exercise of such a power by the legislature can never be necessary. If it be fit and proper that the license should be given to one guardian under particular circumstances to sell the estate of his ward, it is fit and proper that all other guardians should under similar circumstances have the same license. If the jurisdiction of the judges of probate be not sufficiently extensive to reach all proper cases, it may be a good reason why that jurisdiction should be extended, but can hardly be deemed a sufficient reason for the particular interposition of the legislature in an individual case. These cases rest upon the assumption that the exercise of a legislative power must always result in a general act, a rule of general conduct.

In most of the jurisdictions in which it has been held that the power of converting real into personal property is a proper subject for legislative action, it has usually been found convenient to delegate the power of actually ordering the sale to the courts, whose structure better fits them to examine the merits of applications. Proceedings of this character are generally *ex parte*, and afford great opportunity for fraud. Moreover, judicial proceedings, besides being safer, are less expensive. General laws are therefore enacted by the legislatures of most commonwealths delegating this power of authorizing sales in proper cases to the courts.

But, when this power is conferred upon the courts, it does not necessarily become judicial (see next chapter), but may remain ministerial or administrative, requiring discretion and sometimes knowledge of the law. "For aught we see, the same

[1] Jones *vs*. Perry, 10 Yerg. 59.

[2] Opinion of Judges, 4 N. H. 565.

authority might have been given to the selectmen of each town, or to the clerks or registers of the counties."[1] So, whether the general laws are applicable or not to some cases which may arise, or may or may not accomplish all that is desirable, the legislature may nevertheless by special statute grant the permission which, under general laws, would be granted by the courts. Accordingly it is held that, although a general law is in force by which permission might be granted by the courts, it does not deprive the legislature of that full and complete control which it would have possessed, had no statute existed. As has been said, the courts derive their authority to act on the subject from the legislature. The constituent, when he has delegated an authority without an interest, may still do the act himself which he has authorized another to do; and especially is this the case when the constituent is the legislature. The whole authority might be revoked, and the legislature assume the burden itself.[2]

Kentucky, Virginia, Missouri, Oregon, Indiana, Maryland, New Jersey, Arkansas, Florida, Illinois, Wisconsin, Texas, West Virginia, Michigan, and Colorado, obviously regard the exercise of such power by the legislature as improper, since their constitutions forbid the enactment of special laws licensing the sale of lands of minors and other persons under legal disabilities.

Whether the constitutional provisions forbidding special laws in cases where general laws can be made applicable, exclude such special acts as those above considered, has never been decided, but they might be held to do so.[3]

[1] Rice *vs.* Parkman, 16 Mass. 326. [2] *Ibid.*

[3] Cooley's *Const. Limitations*, p. 117 n.

CHAPTER XII

LEGISLATIVE DIVORCES

THE constitutions of Alabama, Arkansas, California, Iowa, Indiana, Maryland, Michigan, Minnesota, Missouri, Nebraska, Oregon, New Jersey, Texas, Wisconsin, Florida, Georgia, Illinois, Kansas, Kentucky, Louisiana, Massachusetts, Mississippi, Nevada, New Hampshire, New York, North Carolina, Ohio, Pennsylvania, Tennessee, Virginia, and West Virginia prohibit legislative divorces. This prohibition accords with the sentiment expressed by all leading jurists, who maintain that the granting of a divorce is not a proper subject for legislative action.[1] Nevertheless, some courts maintain that in the absence of a constitutional prohibition the power of dissolving the matrimonial bond is a proper legislative function.[2]

In England the ecclesiastical courts exercised exclusive jurisdiction over the subject of divorce until the eighteenth century, when their refusal to grant divorces *a vinculo* even in cases of the grossest conjugal delinquency induced applications to parliament. Since that time parliament has exercised the power of granting divorces *a vinculo* for causes supervenient to the marriage. Following this precedent, the colonial and commonwealth legislatures from time to time enacted special laws dissolving the matrimonial bond in special cases. Originally this legislative practice was sustained by the courts on historical grounds. Subsequently it became necessary for

1 Kent's *Commentaries*, vol. 2, p. 96; Bishop on *Marriage, Divorce and Separation*, Sec. 1446.

2 Bishop on *Marriage, Divorce and Separation*, Secs. 1424–1427, 1471.

them to sanction it on grounds of public policy. A long acquiescence in repeated acts of the legislature on particular matters is said to be evidence that those matters have been generally considered by the people as within legislative control.[1] If legislative investigations take place in divorce proceedings, they are no more than those usually made when a change of a law is designed. Furthermore, if jurisdiction is not vested in the judicial tribunals to grant divorce for any cause, cases might arise beyond the jurisdiction of the courts, in which the continuance of the marriage relation would be intolerable, and in which no principle should prevent the legislature from interfering and putting an end to the relation in the interest of the parties thereto, as well as of society. Marriage is not a contract in the ordinary sense of the term. When once formed a relation is created between the parties which they cannot change. It is an institution of society and controlled by public authority. It is a status over which the legislature has complete control. And as marriage is not a contract, an act declaring a dissolution of the tie does not impair the obligations of contracts.[2]

Should such acts now be held unconstitutional, as an encroachment upon the judicial department, the legitimacy of children, the peace of families, and the settlement of estates would be assailed. Such a course would bastardize issue and subject parties to the charge of adultery. Therefore, chiefly to avoid the consequences which would result from declaring those divorces void which have been granted by the legislature, the courts pronounce such divorces valid.[3]

Finally, it is said the fact that the legislature continually exercised this power after the separation of powers, justifies the conclusion that the division of the government into three departments, and the implied inhibition of the legis-

[1] Starr *vs.* Pease, 8 Conn. 541; Maynard *vs.* Hill, 125 U. S. 190.

[2] Magee *vs.* Young, 40 Miss. 164; Maynard *vs.* Hill, 125 U. S. 190.

[3] Bingham *vs.* Miller, 17 Ohio, 445.

lative department to exercise judicial functions, was neither intended nor understood to exclude legislative control over the marriage relation.[1]

But the legislature is limited to the declaration of the divorce; it cannot decide questions of property. A legislative act cannot of its own force turn a divorce *nisi* into an absolute divorce.[2] It has been held that that part of an act of divorce which required the husband to pay to trustees money for the use and benefit of his wife, was void. A suit for alimony is a distinct remedy from proceedings to obtain a divorce, and a wife's maintenance is recoverable only through the intervention of the courts.[3]

Where such act is conceded to be legislative, it follows that the motives of a special law granting the divorce cannot be inquired into by the courts, and the validity of the act is not affected by the fact that it was passed upon the husband's application without the knowledge of or notice to the wife.[4]

It is generally conceded that the determination of the propriety of dissolving a marriage may involve investigations of a judicial nature which can best be conducted by judicial tribunals. Therefore statutes are generally found which authorize courts to decree divorces in certain specified cases. In some jurisdictions it is held that the delegation of authority to the courts to act in certain enumerated cases does not necessarily involve the negation of the reservation of the power to the legislature to act concurrently in the same class of cases, because acts granting the power to the courts may be

[1] Maynard *vs.* Hill, 125 U. S. 190. This case held that a special divorce act of a territorial legislature is a rightful subject of legislation, and not inconsistent with the Constitution of the United States. In 1886 a statute was passed by Congress forbiding special divorce acts by the territorial legislatures (*Stats. of 1886*, ch. 818, sec. 1). See Starr *vs.* Pease, 8 Conn. 541.

[2] Sparhawk *vs.* Sparhawk, 116 Mass. 315.

[3] Crane *vs.* Meginnis, 1 G. & J. (Md.) 463.

[4] Maynard *vs.* Hill, 125 U. S. 190; Wright *vs.* Wright, 2 Md. 429.

repealed at any time.[1] But, in this class of cases, when a competent court has once accepted the jurisdiction and commenced acting on a controversy, the particular matter becomes exclusively judicial, and even though the legislature had an equal authority over it before, it has not now. This is but a branch of the doctrine that between tribunals of concurrent jurisdiction, the one which first takes cognizance of a controversy, can continue it to the end.[2]

A series of cases holds that the power to divorce becomes a judicial act in those cases in which general laws confer on the courts power to adjudicate, and that in those cases the legislature cannot pass special laws, though its original control over the marriage relation will enable it to grant divorces in such other cases as shall in its wisdom appear to justify them.[3] Until the legislature enacts laws on the subject and invests courts with jurisdiction, it can itself exercise the authority at pleasure.[4] But it is powerless over causes of divorce which it has entrusted to the judiciary, else there would practically be an appeal from the highest judicial tribunal to the legislature.[5] The cases, however, generally recognize that, although the legislature has enacted a general law, causes may arise which may make it peculiarly proper to dissolve the marriage relation, but of which the courts could not take cognizance, be-

[1] Wright *vs.* Wright, 2 Md. 429.

[2] Bishop on *Marriage, Divorce and Separation*, Sec. 1448, and cases cited. Divorce may be either a legislative or judicial act. *Id.*, Secs., 1432–1446. If the court acts upon an action for divorce over which it has jurisdiction, and decides against a divorce being granted, parties may not be granted a divorce by the legislature. Op. of Justices, 16 Me. 479.

[3] Levins *vs.* Sleator, 2 Greene (Iowa), 604; Opinion of Judges, 16 Me. 479; Adams *vs.* Palmer, 51 Me. 480; Townsend *vs.* Griffin, 4 Harr. 440. Bishop on *Marriage, Separation and Divorce*, Sec. 1449.

[4] Where courts have no authority by general law to grant a divorce for a given cause, the legislature cannot confer the authority in a particular case. Simmonds *vs.* Simmonds, 103 Mass. 572.

[5] Opinion of Judges, 16 Me. 479; Adams. *vs.* Palmer, 51 Me. 480.

cause not invested with jurisdiction. In such cases it is said to be only proper that the legislature should be able to decree the divorce.

Under the constitution of Pennsylvania, which provides that the legislature shall not have power to enact laws annulling the contract of marriage in any case where by law the courts of the commonwealth are or may be empowered to decree a divorce, it has been decided that this restriction is a recognition of the power of the legislature to grant divorces in all other cases.[1] Under the constitution of Michigan, by which the legislature was prohibited from granting divorces, it was held that a special act could not be passed authorizing the courts to divorce for a cause not embraced in the general laws.[2]

The courts of Ohio, New Hampshire, Florida, Missouri, and Kentucky, have held the granting of a divorce to be in its very nature a judicial act.[3] They maintain that the granting of a divorce is not the enactment of a law. It is a decree, sentence, rule, judgment, but not a law. Nor can the legislature by withholding from the judiciary the means or right of exercising powers properly judicial, by not providing general laws, invest itself with the right of exercising that power.[4]

The conflict of opinion in regard to legislative divorces is exactly analogous to the conflict in regard to special laws authorizing the sale of lands.

[1] Cronise *vs.* Cronise, 54 Pa. St. 255.

[2] Teft *vs.* Teft, 3 Mich. 67.

[3] Bingham *vs.* Miller, 17 Ohio, 445; Clark *vs.* Clark, 10 N. H. 380; Ponder *vs.* Graham, 4 Fla. 23; Gaines *vs.* Gaines, 9 B. Monroe, 295; Bryson *vs.* Bryson, 44 Mo. 232.

[4] Gaines *vs.* Gaines, 9 B. Monroe, 295.

CHAPTER XIII

LEGISLATIVE INQUESTS AND THE POWER TO PUNISH FOR CONTEMPT

As the ascertainment of facts is indispensable to intelligent and effectual legislation, there never has been any question as to the right of the legislature, or of legislators, to make mere naked inquiries. Each house must be allowed to proceed in its own way in the collection of such information as may seem conducive to the discharge of its functions, and, whenever it is deemed desirable that witnesses should be examined, authority to do so is properly given to a committee with such powers of investigation as may seem expedient in the particular case.[1] The manner of conducting such an investigation rests in the sound discretion of the legislature.[2]

In considering this inquisitorial power, the courts have been called upon to determine whether the legislature, in order to make its own inquiries, or those of its committees, effective, has the power of punishing as a contempt a refusal to answer interrogatories. The courts, in determining this question, have unnecessarily confused it by considering whether the power to judge of and to punish for contempt is a power judicial in its nature, and, if so, whether, in view of the separation of governmental powers, it may under any circumstances be exercised by the legislature. Whenever they have upheld the exercise of this power by the legislature, they have deemed it incumbent upon them to justify the exercise by the legislature of a power judicial in its nature, as if the constitution had vested all such power in the courts.

[1] People *vs.* Larned, 5 Hun. 626.

[2] In re Falvey, 7 Wis. 630.

In one of the early cases it was said: "The power is rather judicial in its nature, but in a legislative body exists as an auxiliary to the legislative power only. In the early history of the country from which our institutions, both of law and legislation, are principally derived, the judicial and legislative functions existed in and were exercised by the same body; and when they were afterwards separated, and each came to be exercised by a separate tribunal or body, the legislative authority necessarily retained a sufficient amount of judicial power to enable it to investigate fully and to comprehend thoroughly any and every subject upon which the body proposed to act in its legislative capacity. This included the power to subpœna witnesses to give evidence, to compel them to attend and testify, and to punish for disobedience and contempt in refusing to attend, or in refusing to testify upon attendance."[1]

The provision in the constitutions of Massachusetts[2] and Maryland,[3] declaring that the House of Representatives shall be the Grand Inquest of the commonwealth, would probably be regarded as expressly authorizing the legislature to punish witnesses for contempt in the course of inquiries, investigations or inquests conducted by them or their committees.[4]

In 1821 the United States Supreme Court held that the power of punishing for contempt even others than their own members, was possessed by both houses of Congress by necessary implication. A general power to punish for contempt was held to be vested in the House of Representatives as a neces-

[1] Wilckens *vs.* Willet, 4 Abb. App. Dec. 596. Whenever it is necessary for the legislature to assume powers judicial in their nature in order to exercise powers confided to it by the Constitution, the legislature undoubtedly may exercise such judicial powers. If the legislature may not exercise powers judicial in their nature in other cases, it is not because of the separation of powers, or because judicial power is vested in the courts, but because the legislature has only such powers as the Constitution expressly confers upon it and powers incidental thereto.

[2] Art. 6, sec. 3.

[3] Art. 3, sec. 24.

[4] See Burnham *vs.* Morrisey, 14 Gray, 226.

sary incident to the exercise of its functions, and its adjudication was held sufficient to establish the fact of contempt.[1]

The question was again before the Supreme Court of the United States in 1885. The contempt in this case consisted in a refusal to answer a question propounded by a committee of the House of Representatives. The resolution under which the committee was created directed it to examine into the history and character of what was called "the real estate pool" of the District of Columbia; and the preamble recited as the ground of the investigation that certain debtors of the United States government, whose affairs were then in litigation before a bankruptcy court, had an interest in the pool or were creditors of it.

The court, in deciding the case, said: "The latter proposition [that this power exists as one necessary to enable either house of Congress to exercise successfully its function of legislation] is one which we do not wish to decide in the present case, because we are able to decide it without passing upon the existence or non-existence of such a power in aid of the legislative function." The court further said: "We are sure that no person can be punished for contumacy as a witness before either House unless his testimony is required in a matter into which that House has jurisdiction to inquire, and that neither of these bodies possesses the general power of making an inquiry into the private affairs of the citizens."

The decision denying the legislature the power in that particular case, was based upon the ground that the subject matter of the investigation which the committee was directed to make, was judicial in character, that proceedings to determine it were already before the courts, that the investigation related to a matter wherein no relief or redress could be given by Congress, that the resolution under which the investigation was held contained no indication of any intention of

[1] Anderson *vs.* Dunn, 6 Wheat. 204. See Stewart *vs.* Blaine, 1 MacArthur, 453.

final action by Congress, and that it did not appear what Congress could have done to remedy the wrong. The case decided that in ordering an investigation into business matters in which the national government was interested simply as a creditor of one of the parties, without having for its apparent object any legislative action, the House of Representatives exceeded its authority, and consequently that the committee had no authority to require the plaintiff to testify before it, or to punish him for contempt for refusing to testify. It overruled Anderson against Dunn only so far as the latter held that the resolution of the House finding a person guilty of contempt was conclusive evidence of the fact.[1]

The power of a commonwealth legislature to punish as for contempt the refusal of a witness to testify before its committee, has been thoroughly discussed by the courts of New York.[2] Whereas the constitutions of most commonwealths expressly confer the power to punish for contempt in certain cases upon the legislature,[3] the constitution of New York does not confer such power upon the legislature in a single case. Charges

[1] Kilbourn *vs.* Thompson, 103 U. S. 168. This opinion was rendered by the court in overruling the demurrer of the sergeant-at-arms in an action brought against him by the plaintiff for false arrest and imprisonment. On the first trial of the action in the Supreme Court of the District of Columbia, the plaintiff recovered a verdict for $100,000. A new trial having been granted on the ground that the damages were excessive, he recovered a verdict for $60,000. A third trial was ordered for the same reason, in which the plaintiff recovered a verdict for $37,000. This amount was subsequently reduced to $20,000 by consent, which amount was paid by order of Congress, together with interest and costs of the action. See 23 St. at Large, 427; MacArthur & Mackey, 416–432.

[2] McDonald *vs.* Keeler, 99 N. Y. 463; accord Burnham *vs.* Morrisey, 14 Gray, 226; In re Falvey, 7 Wis. 630; In re Gunn, 50 Kan. 158. In this case the court was called upon to determine which of two rival legislative bodies was the duly organized house. It was insisted that the house which inflicted the penalty was not the properly organized house, since it failed to receive the recognition of the governor and senate. The court, however, held that it, and not its rival, which did receive such recognition, was the proper house, and had power to punish for contempt.

[3] See "Legislative Inquests," by Frederick W. Whitridge, *Pol. Sc. Quarterly*, vol. i, p. 90.

of fraud and irregularity having been publicly made against the Commissioners of Public Works of New York City, the senate adopted a resolution directing and empowering its standing committee on affairs of cities to investigate the charges, and to make a report thereon. The committee executed this mandate pursuant to a general law which provided that each house should have power to punish for contempt any person refusing to attend or to be examined as a witness either before the house or before a committee appointed to take testimony in legislative proceedings.[1] The court, in sustaining the statute, and the proceedings of the senate thereunder, said that the power of obtaining information for the purpose of framing laws to meet supposed or apprehended evils was one which had from time immemorial been deemed necessary and had been exercised by legislative bodies. The court held it unnecessary to consider whether the questions which the relator refused to answer were pertinent, because the contempt charged did not consist in the refusal to answer particular questions, but in the refusal to be further examined, the refusal being based on the ground that the relator's counsel was requested to be withdrawn. In regard to this, it was held that he had no constitutional or legal right to the aid of counsel on such an examination.

The court distinguished the case from Kilbourn against Thompson on the ground that the Department of Public Works was created by statute and was a proper subject for legislative action, and that the committee was directed to report the result of its investigation together with recommendations to the senate for further legislation.

The court also indicated a probable limitation to legislative power in such investigations, which are very liable to abuse. "An investigation instituted for the mere sake of investigation, or for political purposes not connected with intended legislation or with any matters upon which the house could act, but

[1] *Rev. St.*, tit. 2, chap. 7, sec. 1314.

merely intended to subject a party or body investigated to public animadversion, or to vindicate him or it from unjust aspersion, where the legislature had no power to put him or it on trial for supposed offences, and no legislation was contemplated, but the proceeding must necessarily end with the investigation, will not in our judgment be a legislative proceeding, or give to either house jurisdiction to compel the attendance of witnesses or punish them for refusing to attend."

It has also been held that upon the refusal of the clerk of the court of common pleas to produce before a committee any poll-book affecting a contested election, it is lawful for the house from which the committee emanated to order his commitment to jail as for contempt of its authority.[1]

An act creating a state board of tax commissioners with power to send for persons, books, and papers, to hear and question witnesses, has been held void so far as it confers on such officers the power to fine and imprison for contempt. The board belongs to the executive department of the state, and the power to punish for contempt belongs, it was said, *exclusively* to the courts.[2]

Although it is generally conceded that the legislature cannot delegate its power to punish for contempt of its authority, even to its special committee, yet punishment for contempt of the committee, inflicted by the committee itself, was sustained.[3]

The question has been raised as to how far, if at all, the courts may review the action of the legislature in punish-

[1] *Ex parte* Dalton, 43 Ohio St. 142.

[2] Langenberg *vs.* Decker, 31 N. E. 190, and cases cited.

[3] People *vs.* Larned, 5 Hun, 626. The legislature cannot delegate the power to punish for contempt to officers or bodies exercising only administrative powers. People *vs.* Van Tassel, 17 N. Y. 938; Whitcomb's Case, 120 Mass. 118; Langenberg *vs.* Decker, 31 N. E. 190. It seems, however, that it may delegate such power to such officers or bodies when they are acting as a part of the judicial department of the government. Swafford *vs.* Berrong, 10 S. E. 593; In re Daton, 11 S. E. 244; State *vs.* Aiken, 18 S. E. 690; English and American *Law Encyc.*, vol. iii, p. 777.

ing for the contempts herein considered. The question whether an individual has been prejudiced in his rights by the unauthorized assumption of power by any governmental agency, including the legislature, is judicial. The power to determine such a question is part of that judicial power which the constitutions have confided to the courts, and with which the legislature cannot interfere in any manner, as by assuming it itself, or by delegating it elsewhere than to the courts. The duty of determining such a question cannot be shirked by the courts. Accordingly, it has been said that when the court issues the writ of habeas corpus to inquire into the cause of imprisonment, it has the right further to inquire into the matter and determine whether the committing body, even when it is the legislature, or a magistrate, had jurisdiction. But the court has no appellate jurisdiction from or supervisory powers over the proceedings of the legislature in a matter within the constitutional jurisdiction of that body. The legislature, in refusing to hear a petition before adjudging a person in contempt, may have acted arbitrarily and improperly, yet, as the jurisdiction of the assembly acting in such matters is final, and the courts have no appellate power over it, it is not competent for the court to revise the proceedings of the assembly or suspend its judgment because it has made a mistake or abused its discretion in the premises.[1] When the question involved is one of jurisdiction of the committee and house, the question may be reviewed on habeas corpus, and the right of the relator may be determined on such application.[2]

Congress and several of the commonwealth legislatures have by law provided that a person who, being duly summoned to

[1] In re Falvey, 7 Wis. 630.

[2] People, *ex rel.* Sabold, *vs.* Webb, 22 N. Y. St. R. 324, in which case the committal was held to be without jurisdiction and void. "The house of representatives is not the final judge of its own powers and privileges in cases in which the rights and liberties of subjects are concerned; but the legality of its action may be determined by the courts." In re Gunn, 50 Kan. 155.

attend as a witness before either house of the legislature or any committee thereof, authorized to summon witnesses, refuses or neglects, without lawful excuse, to attend pursuant to such summons, or who, being present before either house of the legislature, or any committee thereof, refuses to be sworn or affirmed, and to answer any material or proper question, or to produce upon notice any material and proper books, papers or documents in his possession, or under his control, shall be guilty of a misdemeanor and punishable by the courts.[1]

The power of legislative bodies to punish directly for contempt in refusing to appear as a witness or to answer inquiries of the legislature or its committees is not superseded by such statutes.[2]

The provisions of an act authorizing the Pacific Railway Commission to invoke the aid of any circuit or district court, to require the attendance of witnesses and the production of books, papers and documents relating to the subject of their inquiry, and empowering the courts in case of contumacy or the refusal of persons to obey subpœnas, to issue orders requiring them to appear before the commissioners and present books and papers, if so ordered, and give evidence touching the matters in question, and to punish disobedience to its orders, as a contempt of court, have been deemed unconstitutional. The court observed that " Congress cannot make the courts its instruments in conducting mere legislative investigations; that the courts would thus be mere executors of the commissioners' will, and would be called upon to exercise either administrative functions or judicial power. If the former, they cannot be vested in the courts. If the latter, the

[1] See N. Y. Penal Code, secs. 68–69; 1 N. Y. Rev. St. 154, sec. 13; U. S. Rev. St., secs. 102–104.

[2] People, *ex rel.* McDonald, *vs.* Keeler, 99 N. Y. 463. But in the case of Kilbourn *vs.* Thompson, C. J. Cartter, of the Sup. Ct. of the Dist. of Columbia, in May, 1876, held that as a refusal to testify was an indictable offense by statute, a trial therefor must be had in the courts and not elsewhere. See Cooley's *Const. Limitations*, p. 161 n.

power can only be exercised in cases of controversies enumerated in the constitution, or in cases of habeas corpus."[1]

Proceedings under statutes and resolutions like the foregoing are not trials but investigations. The committees are investigators, inquirers, pursuers, "smellers." Their duties are not judicial but administrative. They are not to hear and decide, but to find out and report. Their proceedings may be kept secret, as were those of the Senate Sugar Scandal Committee of 1894, or made public, as were those of the Lexow Police Department Investigating Committee of 1894. The witnesses before such committees have no legal right to the aid of counsel,[2] nor are such committees bound by the ordinary laws of evidence.[3] But it seems that a witness cannot be compelled to give an answer which might tend to criminate him, unless adequate provision is made that such evidence shall not be used against him in criminal proceedings.[4]

[1] In re Pacific R. Com'n, 32 Fed. Rep. 251. In re McLean, 37 Fed. Rep. 648. The decisions of the Circuit Court holding that Congress cannot make courts instruments in the conduct of mere legislative investigations seem to be inconsistent with a late opinion of the U. S. Supreme Court. That eminent tribunal considered constitutional a provision of a statute which empowered the Circuit Courts of the United States, whenever their aid was invoked by the Interstate Commerce Commission, to order any person or corporation to appear before the Commission and give evidence, and also to punish as a contempt of their authority any failure to obey such orders. The court observed that the provision was not in conflict with the Constitution of the United States as imposing on judicial tribunals duties not judicial in their nature, and that a judgment thereunder was none the less one of a judicial tribunal dealing with questions judicial in their nature, because its effect might be to aid an administrative body in the performance of duties legally imposed upon it by Congress. Interstate Commerce Commission *vs.* Brimson, 154 U. S. 447; Ch. J. Fuller and Judges Jackson and Brewer dissented, 155 U. S. 1.

In Pennsylvania it has been held that the courts may be authorized to procure and present evidence to the legislature in cases of contested elections pending before the legislature, to be acted upon by the legislature as it sees fit. In re McNeill, 111 Pa. St. 235.

[2] *Ex parte* McCarthy, 29 Cal. 395; McDonald *vs.* Keeler, 99 N. Y. 463.

[3] See In re Falvey, 7 Wis. 531.

[4] See People *vs.* Sharp, 107 N. Y. 427; Counselman *vs.* Hitchcock, 142 U. S. 547; In re Falvey, 7 Wis. 630.

The counsel and chairman of the Lexow Committee are reported to have maintained that the removal of a police captain by the police board because of the evidence and admissions of the captain before the committee was "a misuse of the testimony taken before the committee, and a contempt of the Senate of the State of New York." The three police commissioners promptly obeyed the order of the committee and reinstated the police captain.[1]

Many of the questions herein considered will probably soon again be passed upon by the Supreme Court of the United States.

The Grand Jury of the Supreme Court of the District of Columbia indicted several persons for refusing to answer questions relating to alleged campaign contributions by the Sugar Trust in order to secure favorable tariff legislation, which were put to them by a committee of the United States Senate, appointed to investigate the sugar scandals.

During the November Term, 1894, the Supreme Court of the District of Columbia overruled the demurrers to the indictments. The court declared constitutional the statute which provides for the indictment of witnesses refusing to answer questions propounded by Congressional committees. It held that the Senatorial committee had jurisdiction to inquire whether senators had been dealing in stocks of the sugar refining companies, known as sugar stocks, during the pendency of the tariff bill in the senate; also, that in order to confer jurisdiction on the committee, it was not necessary for the resolutions to set forth or avow what final action the Senate had in contemplation upon the information to be obtained. It held it sufficient if it appeared that the Senate had lawful authority to take any legitimate action, unless it also affirmatively appeared upon the face of the resolutions that no final action was contemplated, and that the investigation was carried on simply for the purpose of vindication or animadversion. It held that

[1] See N. Y. daily papers, Dec. 19–22, 1894.

the questions were not such as to call for answers which would criminate the witnesses (stock-brokers), they being as much at liberty to deal with senators as with any one else.[1]

[1] This judgment was subsequently affirmed by the District Court of Appeals. One of the indicted persons was then surrendered by his bail, to enable him to apply to the U. S. Supreme Court for a writ of *habeas corpus*, in which proceeding it was expected the court would pass on the questions at issue. The Supreme Court, however, denied the application for the writ on the ground that it could not interfere in the matter until the case should have been finally disposed of by the district courts.

The executive cannot pardon persons punished by the legislature for contempt of its authority. See Story, vol. 2, p. 337. Post., p. 136.

CHAPTER XIV

JUDICIAL REPUDIATION OF LEGISLATIVE POWERS

NOTWITHSTANDING that the courts have always firmly declined the assumption of legislative powers whenever the legislature has attempted directly to confer such powers upon them,[1] yet in the early history of our judiciary, attempts were made by the courts indirectly to control legislative acts in such a manner as virtually to result in judicial legislation. From their common law right to interpret the law, the courts developed the right to declare statutes void, not only because they violated express limitations, but because they were contrary to the principles of natural justice or of republican government, or because they were repugnant to the intent and spirit of the constitution.[2]

But it is evident that questions of abstract justice, of public policy and state necessity, belong to the legislature, and not to the courts; and for this reason the courts have renounced the power to declare acts of the legislature void, except in cases of unquestionable violation of the constitution.[3] It is the function of the courts to say what the law is, and not what it ought to be. The state has entrusted the law-making power to the discretion of the legislature. Should the courts assume to control this discretion, they would in effect decide whether

[1] See *The Delegation of Powers*, chap. xxi, post.

[2] Warwick *vs* Smith, 5 Paige, 137; People *vs.* Supervisors, 4 Barb. 64; Benson *vs.* Mayor, 10 Barb. 223; Powers *vs.* Bergen, 2 Seld. 358.

[3] Butler *vs.* Palmer, 1 Hill, 324; Kent's *Commentaries*, vol. i, pp. 408, 488; Cochran *vs.* Van Surley, 20 Wend. 381; Sedgwick's *Construction of Statutory and Constitutional Law*, p. 154; People *vs.* Fisher, 24 Wend. 215; State *vs.* Smith, 44 Ohio St. 348; Cooley's *Const. Limitations*, p. 197, *et seq.*

the enactment of that body should or should not be the law. Courts do not, therefore, interfere with matters of legislative discretion.[1] They will not inquire whether acts are expedient or inexpedient, politic or impolitic.[2] So the question whether or not "provision can be made by general law" for a certain purpose is one for the legislature, not for the courts to determine.[3] Where the legislature is empowered "to establish such inferior tribunals from time to time, as it might deem needed," the legislature alone is to judge when the need for such courts has arisen.[4] Whether the use of a new agency (electricity) constitutes a more humane method of inflicting the death penalty than hanging, is a question for the determination of the legislature, and its determination is conclusive upon the courts.[5] Where a clause in a constitution allows the legislature to make "all such laws as may be necessary to carry the constitution into effect," the question of necessity is exclusively determined by the legislature.[6] When the legislature grants a public franchise on the ground of public convenience, the correctness of its judgment as to such convenience cannot be reviewed by the courts.[7]

The constitutional provision[8] vesting in the legislature power to alter senatorial districts, and requiring this to be done so that "each senate district shall contain as nearly as may be an equal number of inhabitants," grants to the legislature a discretion in carrying out the power, and the court has

[1] Malory *vs.* Marietta, 11 Ohio St. 636; State *vs.* Hitchcock, 1 Kan. 178; State *vs.* Boone County Ct., 50 Mo. 317; Patterson *vs.* Barlow, 60 Pa. St. 54.

[2] License Tax Cases, 5 Wall. 462, 469.

[3] State *vs.* Boone County Ct., 50 Mo. 317.

[4] *Ibid.*

[5] People, *ex rel.* Kemmler, *vs.* Durston, 119 N. Y. 569.

[6] State *vs.* Shields, 4 Mo. App. 259.

[7] Fall *vs.* Sutter, 21 Cal. 239. See People *vs.* Kelly, 5 Abb. (N. C.) 383.

[8] N. Y. Const., Art. 3, sec. 4.

no jurisdiction to review the exercise of this discretion unless it appears that it has been plainly and grossly abused.[1]

The motives of the legislature in passing an act cannot be questioned by the courts. The courts must assume that the legislative discretion has been properly exercised.[2]

The judicial department of the United States government will not invade the legislative functions of the commonwealth governments.[3]

[1] People, *ex rel.* Carter, *vs.* Rice, 135 N. Y. 473; compare State *vs.* Cunningham, 51 N. W. 724. It has been suggested that courts should be granted the power of reviewing apportionment acts of the legislature, as a check upon gerrymandering. See "Distrust of Our Law Makers," address of Moorfield Story before Am. Bar Association, N. Y., Aug. 23, 1894.

[2] People *vs.* Lawrence, 36 Barb. 177; People *vs.* New York Central R. R. Co., 34 Barb. 123; Baltimore *vs.* State, 15 Md. 376. See U. S *vs.* Williams, 5 McLean, 135, which holds that the action of Congress on the allowance of a claim against the government is conclusive on the judiciary.

[3] Hine *vs.* Levee Com'rs, 19 Wall. 655. See Rees *vs.* Watertown, 19 Wall. 107. The United States courts will not interfere by injunction with the execution of the registration and election laws of the commonwealths. Green *vs.* Mills, 25 U. S. App. 383.

CHAPTER XV

JUDICIAL LEGISLATION

NOTWITHSTANDING the endeavors of the judiciary to avoid the assumption of legislative power, the English system of judicial interpretation in some cases must inevitably result in judicial legislation.[1] The statutes as curtailed or enlarged by interpretation, and not the bare statutes themselves, become the rule of civil conduct to govern future cases. Where a law is imperfect, but not to such an extent as to render its execution impossible, imperfections in its details may be supplied by rules of court.[2] Although judicial interpretation ought not to curtail or add anything to a statute[3] but only to express the true intention of the legislature, statutes are often so ambiguous that it is impossible to find by rules of construction the intention of the law, and then the judge is called upon to determine what the law should be. The judge thus becomes a legislator. Cases may even arise in which statutes may be construed against their letter.[4] In such cases the judgment of the court may become the creature of an entirely new law fashioned out of existing law.

Whenever a court reverses its own decision, it exercises power legislative as well as judicial in nature.[5] In Hep-

[1] A familiar illustration of judge-made law is the judicial doctrine of prescription. See Angus *vs.* Dalton, 6 Ap. Cas. 740. Sedgwick's *Construction of Statutory and Constitutional Law*, chap. vii, p. 250.

[2] Cochran *vs.* Loring, 17 Ohio, 409.

[3] See "Judge-made Law," in Cooley *On Torts*, p. 12.

[4] See People *vs.* Utica Ins. Co., 15 Johns. 358, 380; Riggs *vs.* Palmer, 115 N. Y. 506; People *vs.* Butler, 147 N. Y. 164.

[5] See Turnpike Co. *vs.* State, 28 Ind. 382.

burn against Griswold,[1] the Supreme Court of the United States held the legal tender acts of Congress unconstitutional. Subsequently, in the Legal Tender Cases,[2] it held them perfectly sound and constitutional. It has been said that if the court had power absolutely to annul an act for unconstitutionality, the first decision destroyed the legal tender acts, and they could not be revived by the second decision of the court without its indulging in the most bare-faced judicial legislation.[3]

It is an indisputable fact that, notwithstanding the separation of powers, the principles and distinctions established by the decision of single cases become a part of the law of the land. Until overriden by express statutes, judicial precedents become a system of rules binding all, and are regarded by the community as the law determining the nature of the obligations contracted under them.[4]

In the absence of statutory provisions or of general rules of court, many rules of practice are developed by judicial legislation.[5] Every court of record has an inherent power to make rules for the transaction of its business.[6] Without this power it would be impossible for courts of justice to dispose of the public business. Delays would be interminable. Every court must therefore have stated rules to go by, and they are the most proper judges of their rules of practice.[7]

It not unfrequently happens that a law authorizes or requires judges to meet and in convention to establish rules of prac-

[1] 8 Wall. 603. [2] 12 Wall. 457.

[3] See Am. Law Rev., March, 1887.

[4] Sedgwick's *Construction of Statutory and Constitutional Law*, chap, vii, p. 250; Ordronaux's *Constitutional Legislation*, p. 408.

[5] Fisher *vs.* Gould, 81 N. Y. 228.

[6] Barry *vs.* Randolph, 3 Binn. 277. See N. Y. Code of Civil Procedure, sec. 7; Baldwin *vs.* Mayor, 42 Barb. 549, aff'd in 45 Barb. 359.

[7] Snyder *vs.* Bauchman, 8 S. & R. (Pa.) 336; Fullerton *vs.* Bank of U. S., 1 Pet. 604.

tice and procedure which shall be binding upon all courts of record, except courts for the trial of impeachments or superior courts.[1] The rules established by the convention of judges[2] have the force and effect of statutes that cannot be properly departed from.[3] A right secured by a rule so adopted is one of which a party cannot be deprived except by legislation or revision.[4] A rule of court (in the absence of legislation) can be abolished only by the authority of the court, in the same manner as it was made. It cannot remain as a rule of court and at the same time be considered as abolished by an order of the judge, resting only in parol.[5]

It is competent for the judges in convention to make rules altering the practice previously settled by the decisions of the courts.[6] A valid rule may be abolished by the legislature in express terms annulling it, or ordaining something contrary in effect to it.[7] A court may sometimes under special circumstances suspend its rules, or except a particular case from them, to subserve the ends of justice.[8]

The delegated power of the judges in convention to make rules of practice resembles in every respect legislation. Such a rule of practice differs from a statute only in that it is not enacted by the legislature, but by the court. It is somewhat analogous to the delegated ordinance power of the executive.

This power must be considered as essential to the existence

[1] N. Y. Code of Civ. Pro., secs. 17, 193, 323; L. 1882, chap. 410, sec. 1558; N. Y. Law Journal, Nov. 24, 1894.

[2] The legislatures may establish such rules and regulations, or delegate the power of establishing them to the courts. See Wayman *vs.* Southard, 10 Wheat. 1.

[3] People *vs.* Nichols, 18 Hun, 530, 535; reversed in 79 N. Y. 582, but only on another point; Matter of Moore, 108 N. Y. 280; Pratt *vs.* Pratt, 32 N. E. 747.

[4] People *vs.* Nichols, 18 Hun, 530. See Kelly *vs.* Sheehan, 76 N. Y. 325.

[5] Burlington R. R. Co. *vs.* Marchand, 5 Iowa, 468.

[6] Havemeyer *vs.* Ingersoll, 12 Abb. Pr. (N. S.) 301.

[7] Bishop *vs.* State, 30 Ala. 344.

[8] U. S. *vs.* Breitling, 20 How. 252; Gillette Mfg. Co. *vs.* Ashton, 56 Neb. 576.

of the courts, as a power having always been exercised by the courts, and therefore not within the intention of the restriction of the distributing clause of the constitutions.

Since the constitutions do not authorize the legislature to delegate any law-making power proper to a convention of judges, the courts cannot make general rules inconsistent with the code enacted by the legislature. In such case the courts would be enacting a law.[1] A rule in conflict with a statute is of no effect.[2] A rule intended to operate retrospectively as an act of limitations, is void. Statutes of limitation can be modified only by the legislature.[3]

[1] Winton *vs.* English, 14 Abb. Pr. (N. S.) 124, 125; Gormerly *vs.* McGlynn, 84 N. Y. 284; French *vs.* Powers, 80 N. Y. 146; Rice *vs.* Ehele, 55 N. Y. 518; Glenney *vs.* Stedwell, 64 N. Y. 120.

[2] People *vs.* Bruff, 9 Abb. (N. C.) 153.

[3] Reist *vs.* Heilbrenner, 11 S. & R. (Pa.) 131.

PART IV

THE LEGISLATURE AND THE EXECUTIVE

CHAPTER XVI

THE PARDONING POWER

As to what powers should be included in the term executive as that term is used in the distributing clause of the constitutions, the opinions of judges are in conflict; but all agree that whatever power or duty is expressly imposed upon the executive department becomes executive in the sense that it is altogether free from the interference of the other branches of the government. Especially is this the case where the subject is committed to the discretion of the chief executive officer, either by the constitution or by statute. As long as a power is vested in him, it is to be by him exercised, and no other branch of the government can control its exercise.[1] This principle is readily applied to the cases in which the constitutions vest certain powers in the executive officers. Its application to such cases is well established and illustrated by

[1] Att'y Gen'l *vs.* Brown, 1 Wis. 442. Groom *vs.* Gwinn, 43 Md. 572, holds that, although the governor is vested by the constitution with jurisdiction to decide cases of contested elections for attorney general, the power thus conferred is not self-executing, and that it cannot be exercised by the governor until he is clothed by law with authority and means to execute it, as with authority to summon witnesses, to compel their attendance, to punish their refusal to attend, and to administer oaths.

Where the governor is made the commander-in-chief of the military forces of the commonwealth, it is generally admitted that his authority must be exercised under such rules as the legislature may prescribe.

decisions relative to the pardoning power, and to the power of remitting fines and forfeitures.

When the power to remit fines and forfeitures is confided by the constitution to the governor alone, any act of the legislature which attempts directly or indirectly to remit a fine, either before or after it has been paid, is unconstitutional.[1] The legislature cannot relieve persons from penalties incurred by the violation of certain penal statutes.[2] It has even been held that where the constitution confers upon the governor power to remit fines and forfeitures and to grant reprieves, commutations, and pardons, the legislature cannot authorize a court, or a judge thereof, on an appeal from a judgment of conviction, to suspend the sentence of death.[3]

In the absence of constitutional limitations, the legislature could, without doubt, confer upon the courts authority to grant pardons or reprieves. The pardoning power is not a power which necessarily inheres in the executive;[4] and when the constitution is silent, it does not belong to one branch of the government more than to another. That the governor is generally granted this power is the result of history.[5] But, where the constitution grants the power to the governor, the legislature cannot confer it upon any other person or tribunal.[6] Nor can a judge practically exercise the governor's power of pardon by suspending sentence indefinitely.[7] Nor can the legislature limit or restrict the executive's power to pardon.[8] A legislative enactment signed by the governor, remit-

[1] Haley *vs.* Clark, 26 Ala. 439.

[2] State *vs.* Sloss, 25 Mo. 291.

[3] Butler *vs.* State, 97 Ind. 373.

[4] State *vs.* Nichols, 26 Ark. 74.

[5] Lieber, *Civil Liberty and Self-Government*, vol. 2, 147.

[6] Sterling *vs.* Drake, 29 Ohio St. 457; State *vs.* Nichols, 26 Ark. 74; Ogletree *vs.* Dozier, 59 Ga. 300.

[7] People *vs.* Brown, 54 Mich. 15.

[8] U. S. *vs.* Klein, 13 Wall. 128; Armstrong *vs.* U. S., *Id.* 154; Paryond *vs.* U. S., *Id.* 156.

ting the sentence imposed in a criminal case, was regarded as equivalent to a pardon signed by the governor.[1]

It should be noticed that where a judgment in favor of the government involves the property of the government, it can be released by the legislature on any conditions which it chooses to prescribe. The legislature would have the same right to discharge it as it would have to release any debtor of the government from his obligation.[2]

The modification of penalties by statute is not, as a general rule, considered an interference with the pardoning power.[3]

The Secretary of the Treasury may be authorized to remit penalties for the breach of revenue and similar laws,[4] as penalties incurred by a steamship carrying too many passengers.

The pardoning power is generally understood to extend to all cases except impeachments. Under the liberal construction applied to the clause conferring this power upon the chief executive, it has been held that the exception proves the comprehensive nature of the power. The executive has the power to grant conditional pardons to take effect upon conditions either precedent or subsequent,[5] and the power to pardon may be exercised before as well as after conviction.[6] It has also been decided that the chief executive may grant a conditional pardon to a person under sentence of death, commuting that punishment into imprisonment for life, although it was argued that the executive granting such a pardon legislated a new punishment into existence, and then sentenced the convict to suffer it.[7] Though the warrant of a governor

[1] People *vs.* Stewart, 1 Idaho, (N. S.) 546. [2] People *vs.* Bircham, 12 Cal. 50.

[3] Commonwealth *vs.* Halloway, 42 Pa. St. 446, 448; *Ex parte* Scott, 19 Ohio St. 581.

[4] The *Laura*, 114 U. S. 411.

[5] Lee *vs.* Murphy, 22 Gratt. 789; United States *vs.* Wilson, 7 Peters, 150; *Ex parte* Marks, 64 Cal. 29; Kennedy's Case, 135 Mass. 48.

[6] Dominick *vs.* Bowdoin, 44 Ga. 357.

[7] *Ex parte* Wells, 18 How. (U. S.) 307.

speaks of commuting punishment, if it substitutes a less for a greater penalty, and this is intended to be done with the consent of the prisoner, it will be considered a conditional pardon, and not a commutation, the governor having full power to pardon, but power to commute only capital punishment.[1]

It is generally held that the power to pardon includes the power to reprieve. It has been said: "The governor has the unlimited and unrestricted power to pardon, and upon the principle that the greater includes the less, must be held to have authority to postpone the execution of a sentence while engaged in the consideration of the question of exercising the pardoning power."[2] But the power to reprieve is not derived exclusively from the power to pardon. Courts cannot pardon, but courts may stay execution and may reprieve at common law; the power of reprieving is also vested in the governor *ex necessitate legis*. Cases, as of insanity, might arise when courts are not in session, which, although affording no grounds for pardon, yet ought to be reprieved.[3]

The power of the courts to suspend sentence does not conflict with the power vested by the constitution in the governor to grant reprieves and pardons.[4]

Since a contempt of court is an offence against the state and not an offence against the judge personally, the order of the judge inflicting a penalty for such contempt comes within the range of the pardoning prerogative vested by the constitution in the executive.[5] The President of the United States is also held to be clothed with the power of granting pardons in cases where judges of the United States courts punish for contempt.[6]

[1] Lee *vs.* Murphy, 22 Gratt. 789. [2] *Ex parte* Fleming, 60 Miss. 910.

[3] *Ex parte* Howard, 17 N. H. 545. [4] People *vs.* Ct. of Sessions, 141 N. Y. 288.

[5] State *vs.* Sauvinet, 24 La. Ann. 119; *Ex parte* Hickey, 4 Smedes & Marshall, 751.

[6] 4 Op. of Att'y Gen'l, 458; *In re* Mullee, 7 Blatchf. 24. These decisions suggest the question how far the executive might interfere with the courts by pardon-

In conclusion it only remains to be stated that Kansas, Florida, Alabama, Arkansas, Texas, Mississippi, Oregon, Indiana, Iowa and Virginia provide by their constitutions that the foregoing powers shall only be exercised by the governor under such regulations as shall be prescribed by law.[1]

In the absence of constitutional provision, statutes regulating the manner of making an application for pardon are merely directory, and do not limit the power of the governor to pardon to cases in which application is made as therein provided, nor is the effect of such statutes enlarged by the usual constitutional provision that the governor may grant the pardon, but that the legislature may by law regulate the manner of the application.[2]

ing persons committed by a judge for the purpose of coercion, as in the case of a contumacious witness. See *The Laura*, 114 U. S. 411. There is some authority for the proposition that the executive cannot pardon persons under sentence by the legislature for contempt of its authority. 2 Story on the Constitution, 337. It is at least questionable whether a distinction should be made between the power of the executive to pardon a contempt of court and a contempt of the legislature.

[1] See State *vs.* Dunning, 9 Ind. 20.

[2] *In re* Moore, 31 Pac. R. 980. See Governor *vs.* Warden, 62 N. Y. 584; N. W. Law Journal, April 24, 1895.

CHAPTER XVII

THE POWER OF APPOINTMENT AND REMOVAL

A PHASE of the relations existing between the legislature and the executive is illustrated by the law of appointment and removal.

A provision generally found in the commonwealth constitutions declares that the governor shall nominate and, by and with the consent of the senate, appoint all officers whose offices are established by the constitution or shall be created by law, *and whose appointment or election is not otherwise provided for.*

This clause has received different constructions in the several commonwealths. The conflict in the decisions arises from the difficulty encountered in the construction and interpretation of the distributing clause. Does the term executive, as employed in this clause, include all powers generally termed executive in their nature, or does the enumeration of certain powers which the constitution expressly vests in the chief executive, imply that the state only intended to include in its grant of the executive powers to the executive department such powers as are expressly enumerated? If the state intended to vest in the governor all powers executive in their nature, what was its purpose in specifying particular executive acts which he might lawfully exercise?

It has been held that while the above provision authorizes the legislature to provide for appointment or election to office, it does not authorize that body itself to make such appointment or election. It is one thing to make a place by enacting a law, and another thing to put a person in that place. The one thing is purely and intrinsically legislative, the other is not. For these reasons, a law effecting an appointment of the board of public works and affairs has in Indiana been held to be invalid.[1] But, in the same commonwealth, although it has subsequently been affirmed that appointment is an executive act and that the legislature has no power to fill offices except such as are connected with the discharge of legislative duties, it has been decided that the assembly, having since the adoption of the constitution uniformly assumed the power of appointing or directing the appointment of officers of benevolent institutions of the commonwealth, in which assumption all departments have apparently acquiesced, is authorized to appoint a trustee of the Institution for the Blind. Benevolent institutions were said to be the property of the commonwealth, and as such under the general control of the legislature.[2] When subsequently the Indiana legislature established a department of geology to be under the direction of a director, and the legislature elected the director, the courts declared that, the legislature having created the office, but having had no power to fill it, or to delegate that power, it being executive in its nature, and therefore inhering in the executive department of government, the office became vacant as soon as created, and that therefore the governor had the right to fill the vacancy.[3]

Although the constitution has confided to the courts the appointment of their own clerks, it has been decided that the nature of the power is not changed. The act does not become judicial, but remains intrinsically executive, and therefore neither an appeal nor a writ of error will lie to the courts to review, reverse, or nullify it.[4]

The authorities which hold that the power of appointment is executive avoid great difficulty by declaring that though the

[1] State *vs.* Denny, 21 N. E. Rep. 252.

[2] Governor *vs.* State, 21 N. E. Rep. 890.

[3] State *vs.* Hyde, 121 Ind. 20.

[4] Taylor *vs.* Commonwealth, 3 J. J. Marsh. 401. Explained in Mayor *vs.* State, 15 Md. 376.

appointment to office is an act executive in its nature, yet not every such appointment involves executive functions, as appointments by judicial officers in the discharge of their duties, or appointments by the legislature in the discharge of its duties as an independent body. Such appointments are necessary to maintain the independent existence of the departments, and are not an encroachment upon the executive department.[1]

That nomination to office is an executive act was earnestly maintained by Thomas Jefferson. In one of his letters he says: "Nomination to office is an executive function. To give it to the legislature as we do, is a violation of the principle of the separation of powers. It swerves members from correctness by temptation to contract for office for themselves and to a corrupt barter for votes, and destroys responsibility by dividing it among a multitude. By leaving nomination in its proper place among executive functions, the principle of the distribution of powers and responsibility weighs with its heaviest force upon a single head."[2]

On the other hand, a large majority of decided cases maintain the view that all the powers usually denominated executive by theoretical writers, were not intended to be included in the grant to the governor of the executive power, and that the enumeration of specific powers which the executive might exercise was intended to operate as a limitation of the general grant.[3] The power of appointment to office is not generally, under any system of checks and balances, regarded as a function intrinsically executive in the sense that it is inherent in and necessarily belongs to the executive department.[4] Webster says:[5] "First, the denomination of a department does not fix the limit of the powers conferred on it, *nor even their exact*

[1] State *vs.* Denny, 21 N. E. Rep. 252; State *vs.* Hyde, 30 Am. and Eng. Corp. Cases, 318, 321 n, and 334 n.

[2] Field *vs.* The People, 3 Ill. 79, 141.

[3] *Ibid.*, 79.

[4] Mayor *vs.* State, 15 Md. 376.

[5] Speech on "Presidential Protest."

nature; and second (which indeed follows from the first), in our American government, the chief executive magistrate does not necessarily, and by force of his general character of supreme executive, possess the appointing power."

Where this view of the distributing clause prevails, it has been held that under a constitutional provision like the one above considered, the legislature may, in cases not provided for by the constitution, prescribe by general law the manner in which all public officers shall be elected or appointed, and that this power includes the power to designate the agent or person who shall appoint as well as the formality with which it shall be done. Were a literal construction of the clause in question to be insisted upon, the time of the senate would be taken up in acting upon the governor's nominations.[1] Where the appointment is to a statutory office, it is competent for the legislature to provide in a different way than that proposed by the constitution, the manner of making original appointments, the terms of office and how all vacancies shall be filled.[2] Vesting the executive power of the commonwealth in the governor does not include the power to fill vacancies in offices created by act of the legislature.[3]

The legislature may provide for the appointment of a civil service commission to make rules and regulations to govern the qualifications and appointment of all statutory officers.[4] But the constitution of New York, for the purpose of fixing responsibility, confers on the Superintendent of Public Works of the state power to select and appoint his subordinates. This, it has been held, gives him exclusive power in his appointments, so that the civil service statute, so far as it attempts to restrict him in his choice to persons certified to him by commissioners, is unconstitutional.[5]

[1] Bridges *vs.* Shallcross, 6 W. Va. 562. [2] People *vs.* Osborne, 7 Col. 605.

[3] Briggs *vs.* McBride, 17 Ore. 9.

[4] Opinions of Justices, 138 Mass. 601. "This is not the delegation of power to enact laws; it is merely a delegation of administrative powers and duties."

[5] People *vs.* Angle, 109 N. Y. 564.

The legislature, having power to prescribe the rule of selection, whether it shall be by election or appointment, may itself make the selection.[1] So, for the legislature to name, in an act of incorporation of a city, trustees to organize the city government and conduct its affairs through the first year, is not regarded as an assumption of executive powers.[2] To avoid legislative appointments, provisions are frequently inserted into the constitutions, declaring that no appointing power shall be exercised by the general assembly, except as prescribed in the constitution.[3]

Where the question, whether an officer shall be elected or appointed, is left to the discretion of the general assembly, a law directing his election or appointment may be changed at the will of the legislature.[4] The legislature may withdraw the power of appointment to statutory office from the governor[5] and vest it in any administrative board or officer.[6] And in New York it has been held that the power of appointment may be granted to unofficial persons,[7] as chambers of commerce and presidents of insurance companies.

The legislature may change the time of the election of the successor of an officer, so as to prolong the term of such officer till a successor is appointed. This does not amount to a legislative appointment to office.[8] In the absence of express constitutional prohibitions, where a particular office has been created by statute, the legislature may, in its discretion, abolish the office without regard to the tenure or expectations of the incumbent.[9] It may pass an act lengthening or abridging the

[1] Mayor *vs.* State, 15 Md. 376; People *vs.* Freeman, 22 Pac. Rep. 173.

[2] State *vz.* Rosenstock, 11 Nev. 128.

[3] Bridges *vs.* Shallcross, 6 W. Va. 562; State *vs.* Kennon, 7 Ohio St. 546.

[4] State *vs.* Covington, 29 Ohio St. 102; People *vs.* Draper, 15 N. Y. 532.

[5] Davis *vs.* State, 7 Md. 151.

[6] People *vs.* Shallcross, 6 W. Va. 562.

[7] Sturgis *vs.* Spofford, 45 N. Y. 446.

[8] People *vs.* Batchelor, 22 N. Y. 128.

[9] State *vs.* Hermann, 11 Mo. App. 43; Bryan *vs.* Cattell, 15 Ia. 538.

term of such an officer.[1] It may declare such office vacant and appoint another person to fill the vacancy.[2]

When the constitution confers the power of appointment to or removal from office upon the executive department alone, it is evident that such appointment or removal cannot be made directly or indirectly by legislative enactment.[3] It has been held that a constitutional right of the appointing power to remove at pleasure cannot be abridged by an act providing for the removal in a certain way or for a certain cause.[4] Although a statute which provides for a board, authorizing it to appoint or remove officers, or to fill vacancies, is valid, and although the legislature cannot appoint the officers of such board without exercising the power of appointment,[5] yet where the legislature creates a board of public works of which certain officers of the state are *ex officio* the members, and authorizes such board to appoint to or remove from office, or to fill vacancies, such act does not operate as a legislative appointment to another or different office, but only annexes additional powers and duties to be performed by persons already elected by the people. It does not amount to a legislative appointment to an office created by law.[6]

The Constitution of the United States requires certain officers to be appointed by the President by and with the advice and consent of the Senate.[7] But as, when officers become numerous and sudden removals necessary, inconveniences might otherwise arise, it is provided that Congress may by

[1] Territory *vs.* Pyle, 1 Ore. 149.

[2] People *vs.* Barnard, 27 Cal. 470; Att'y Gen'l *vs.* Squires, 14 Cal. 13; Bryan *vs.* Cattell, 15 Ia. 538.

[3] Hood *vs.* United States, 15 Ct. of Cl. 151.

[4] People *vs.* Hill, 7 Cal. 97.

[5] State *vs.* Kennon, 7 Ohio St. 546.

[6] Bridges *vs.* Shallcross, 6 W. Va. 562.

[7] Generally the President and the governors are empowered to fill all vacancies happening during the recess of the Senate. U. S. Const., art. 2, sec. 2. This provision is regarded as applying to vacancies happening during the session and continuing after adjournment. *In re* Farrows, 4 Woods (C. C.) 491; State *vs.* Kuhl, 17 Atl. Rep. 102.

law vest the appointment of other officers in the President alone, in courts of law, or in the heads of departments. Congress, however, has no power to confer authority to appoint to office upon any persons not named to that end in the Constitution.[1]

Although the Constitution of the United States is silent as to the whereabouts of the general power of removal from office, Congress in 1789 affirmed that it was vested in the President, as a power executive in its nature and indispensable to a due execution of the laws and the regular administration of public affairs. This was acquiesced in as the true construction of the Constitution until the passage by Congress from political motives of the Tenure of Office Act of March 2, 1867, which made the consent of the Senate necessary to the removal of civil officers, even of the heads of the several departments. This act was greatly modified on April 5, 1869, and was with general approval repealed in 1887. It remains doubtful whether the President has the sole power of removal by virtue of the Constitution or by virtue of the act of Congress.[2]

The commonwealths have placed a similar construction upon their constitutional provisions, and hold that the fact that the consent of the senate is necessary to authorize the governor to appoint does not prohibit him from removing officers at his pleasure.[3] But there are some decisions to the contrary. On the ground that the power of removal is incident to the power of appointment, it has been held that an officer cannot be removed by the governor without the consent of the senate, where he is to hold during the pleasure of the power appointing him.[4]

[1] United States *vs.* Germain, 99 U. S. 508.

[2] Story's *Commentaries on the Constitution*, vol. 2, p. 363.

[3] Wilcox *vs.* People, 90 Ill. 186; Lane *vs.* Commonwealth, 103 Pa. St. 481; Harman *vs.* Harwood, 58 Md. 1; Keenan *vs.* Perry, 24 Tex. 253; People *vs.* Hill, 7 Cal. 97.

[4] People *vs.* Freese, 83 Cal. 453. See Field *vs.* People, 3 Ill. 82.

CHAPTER XVIII

IMPLIED AND INCIDENTAL POWERS OF THE EXECUTIVE DEPARTMENT

SINCE the manner in which a statute is to be executed may properly be made a part of a statute, it follows that in many cases, whether the executive shall have discretionary power or act merely ministerially in the execution of laws depends largely upon the will of the legislature. But the executive department, in the execution of its duties, constitutional as well as statutory, is often compelled to exercise its discretion. While it is limited in the exercise of its power by the law, it does not follow that it must show a specific provision for everything it does. No government could attempt to regulate by law the minute movements of every part of its complicated machinery. While the great outlines of its movements may be marked out, and limitations imposed on the exercise of its powers, there are numberless things, essential to its proper action, which can neither be anticipated nor defined.[1]

The quasi-legislative power of the President as commander-in-chief of the army and navy to establish rules and regulations for the government of the army is undoubted. The Secretary of War being the regular constitutional organ of the President for the administration of the military establishment of the nation, the rules and regulations publicly promulgated through him must be received as the acts of the executive, and as such are binding upon all within the sphere of his legal and

[1] United States *vs.* Macdaniel, 7 Peters, 1.

constitutional authority, and cannot be questioned or defied because they may be thought unwise or mistaken.[1]

The governor, as the proper representative of the commonwealth government, is bound to protect its interests. Therefore, in a case where the attorney general, or other officer, is absent from the commonwealth, or fails to discharge his duties, as in taking an appeal, the governor is bound to intervene in behalf of the government and take the appeal.[2]

Although there is no express statute authorizing it, yet the President of the United States has authority to direct a United States marshal to accompany and protect from a threatened assault a Justice of the Supreme Court while in the discharge of his duties, it being the President's duty to see that the laws are executed.[3]

On the same ground the executive department may appoint commissioners and agents to make investigations required by acts or resolutions of Congress, although it cannot pay them except from appropriations for that purpose.[4]

Any power which is not constitutionally vested in one of the departments, or in some particular authority, and which the legislature may delegate, it may vest in the executive, either alone or in conjunction with some other authority. For instance, it may provide that the price to be given for lands

[1] United States *vs.* Eliason, 16 Pet. 291, 301. See U. S. *vs.* Freeman, 3 How. (U. S.) 556.

It having been made the duty of the Secretary of the Treasury from time to time to establish rules and regulations not inconsistent with the laws of the United States, to secure a faithful appraisal of all goods and merchandise imported into the United States, his decision is binding and conclusive upon all the collectors and other officers of the customs, whenever a difficulty arises as to the true construction of the revenue laws. Sampson *vs.* Peaslee, 20 How. 571.

[2] State *ex rel.* Mahan *vs.* Dobuclet, 22 La. Ann. 602. See Stephenson *vs.* Little, 10 Mich. 433.

[3] *In re* Neagle, 135 U. S. 1; C. J. Fuller and Lamar, J., dissenting.

[4] 4 Op. Att'y Gen'l, 248.

condemned for public use, shall be subject to the approval of the President as well as of commissioners.[1]

Congress has frequently delegated to the President discretionary administrative powers of a far-reaching nature.

The alien act of July 6, 1798, vested in the President power to order such aliens as he should adjudge dangerous to the peace and safety of the United States, or should have reasonable grounds to suspect were concerned in any treasonable or secret machinations against the government, to depart from the territory of the United States within such time as should be expressed in his order. This act was very unpopular, because it was said to unite legislative and judicial powers with the executive powers of the President.

An act authorizing the President to establish by proclamation or other public acts, rules and regulations for apprehending, restraining, securing and removing alien enemies, was regarded as necessarily conferring upon him all powers for enforcing such orders. It was held that it was unnecessary for him to call in the aid of the judiciary to enforce such regulations, and that the courts should make the ordinances of the President the rule of their decisions.[2]

The making by the President of rules and regulations for calling forth and drafting the militia is not the exercise of a power strictly and exclusively legislative, and an act of Congress giving the President power to make all necessary rules and regulations to carry into effect the law for calling out the militia, is not the delegation of the legislative powers of Congress, although Congress could have exercised the power it delegated.[3]

Recently the Supreme Court of the United States, in

[1] Shoemaker *vs.* United States, 147 U. S. 281.

[2] Lockington *vs.* Smith, 1 Peters' C. C. 466.

[3] *In re* Griner, 16 Wis. 423. For good illustrations of the exercise of the ordinance power, see Jones *vs.* United States, 137 U. S. 202; Goodnow's *Adm. Law*, vol. 2, pp. 30, 40, 44, 106.

upholding the validity of the reciprocity clause of the McKinley act, rendered a decision of great importance. The court held that Congress has the power to delegate to the President of the United States the power by proclamation at a future day to revoke or modify certain clauses of an act. A close examination of the dissenting opinions of Chief Justice Fuller and Justice Lamar will reveal the fact that they do not disagree with the principles of law applied by the majority ot the court, but rather with their interpretation of the meaning of the words of the act.

The reciprocity clause provided: "With a view to procure reciprocal trade with countries producing the following articles, and for this purpose, *whenever and so often as the President shall be satisfied* that the government of any country producing and exporting sugar, molasses, coffee, tea, hides, or any other article, imposes duties or other exactions upon the agricultural or other products of the United States, which, in view of the free introduction of such sugar, molasses, coffee, tea, or hides into the United States, *he may deem to be reciprocally unequal and unreasonable*, he shall have the power, and it *shall be his duty to suspend*, by proclamation to that effect, the provisions of the act relating to the free introduction of such sugar, molasses, coffee, tea, or hides, the products of such country, *for such time as he shall deem just*, and in such case and during such suspension, duties shall be collected and paid upon such products from such country."

A majority of the court held that the statute vested no discretionary power in the President; that, when he ascertained the fact that duties reciprocally unequal and unreasonable were imposed upon certain products of the United States by a country exporting sugar, molasses, coffee, tea, or hides, it became his *duty* to issue a proclamation declaring a suspension of privileges as to that country; and that, in ascertaining the fact and issuing his proclamation, he did not exercise the function of making laws. He was the mere agent of the law making department to ascertain and declare the event upon which its expressed will was to take effect. This construction of the act brought it within the rulings of the Supreme Court on the Non-Intercourse Acts of 1809 and 1810,[1] in respect of which it was held that Congress might make their suspension or revival depend upon the proclamation of the President, based upon the ascertainment by him of the fact that the edicts of certain nations had been so revoked or modified that they did or did not violate the neutral rights of the United States. An uninterrupted acquiescence in numerous precedents of similar legislation was also regarded by the court as further evidence of the constitutionality of the reciprocity clause. During Washington's administration, Congress authorized the President, at times when Congress was not in session, "*whenever in his opinion* the public safety shall so require," to lay an embargo.[2] During Madison's administration, the President was authorized to repeal certain duties "*when the President of the United States shall be satisfied*" that duties of foreign nations discriminating against the United States had been abolished.[3]

Chief Justice Fuller and Mr. Justice Lamar, in their dissenting opinions as to the constitutionality of the clause in question, maintain that it transfers to the President legislative power, that it deputes to him the power to suspend another section in the same act "*whenever he may deem*" acts of foreign nations reciprocally unequal, and that it further deputes to him the power to continue that suspension and to impose revenue duties "*for such time as he may deem just*," and thus attempts to clothe the executive with discretionary powers which the Constitution has vested in the law-making depart-

[1] Brig *Aurora vs.* United States, 7 Cranch, 382. Schooner Anne *vs.* United States, Id. 570.

[2] 1 St. 372.

[3] 3 St. 224. A summary of analogous laws, and proclamations made under them, is contained in the decision and reporter's note.

ment. These features, they say, distinguish the act in question from the legislative precedents, none of which, excepting the Non-Intercourse Acts, had undergone review by the Supreme Court, or been sustained by its decision, and which, if really precedents, could not avail as authority against a clear and undoubted principle of the Constitution.[1]

If dire necessity should ever require it, the precedents of our Civil War will probably be adduced as authority for the proposition that the war power of the President includes the power to assume the functions of all three departments. Once, at least, the state regarded the President as justified in breaking the Constitution in order to preserve it. By virtue of his war powers, President Lincoln by his Emancipation Proclamations[2] of 1862 and 1863 established a law as effectively as any ever passed by a legislature.[3] By his proclamation suspending the writ of habeas corpus without any previous legislative sanction, he assumed powers legislative and judicial.[4]

Although the courts have indicated that the President has no authority to suspend the writ of habeas corpus, except when and as authorized by Congress, because its suspension involves the exercise of legislative power, they upheld the action of the President in suspending the writ by a proclamation in pursuance of a statute[5] which, during the late Civil War, did

[1] Field *vs.* Clark, 143 U. S. 649.

[2] The executive's power to issue proclamations admonishing citizens of their own duties and responsibilities as an incidental power, though formerly questioned, is now firmly established. Story's *Com. on the Const.*, vol. 2, p. 387.

[3] Shaback *vs.* Cushman, 12 Fla. 472; Dorris *vs.* Grace, 24 Ark. 326; Morgan *vs.* Nelson, 43 Ala. 586; Hall *vs.* Keen, 31 Tex. 504.

[4] "The Constitution of the United States in Civil War," *Political Science Quarterly*, vol. i, p. 163. "The Suspension of the Habeas Corpus during the War of the Rebellion," *Political Science Quarterly*, vol. iii, p. 345. See *Ex parte* Merryman, Taney's Decisions; McCall *vs.* McDowell, 1 Abb. (U. S.) 212; *Ex parte* Field, 5 Blatch. (U. S. Cir.) 63; *In re* Kemp, 16 Wis. 539; Griffin *vs.* Wilcox, 21 Ind. 370.

[5] 13 St. at Large, 730.

not declare a general suspension of the writ, but empowered the President to exercise his judgment and supersede it in particular cases as he might deem the public interest required.[1]

Many executive war measures, legislative in their nature, were sustained by the courts. The president's order authorizing the arrest wherever found within the jurisdiction of the United States, of persons absenting themselves to avoid being drafted, was declared to be a legal and valid order.[2]

In time of war, if portions of hostile territory are in military occupation, the President, as commander-in-chief, may appoint provisional courts for the determination of controversies within such territory.[3]

Nor was the appointment by the President of provisional governors over the commonwealths in revolt, until in pursuance of acts of Congress their governments could be reconstructed, the exercise of unconstitutional powers.[4]

[1] McCall *vs.* McDowell, 1 Abb. (U. S.) 212. See *Ex parte* Field, 5 Blatch. 63.

[2] Allen *vs.* Colby, 47 N. H. 544. See Jones *vs.* Seward, 40 Barb. 563.

[3] Jackson *vs.* Montgomery, 13 How. 498; The *Grapeshot*, 9 Wall. 129. See Edwards *vs.* Tanneret, 12 Wall. 446; Mechanics' Bk. *vs.* Union Bk., 22 Wall. 276.

[4] See Texas *vs.* White, 7 Wall. 730.

PART V

THE EXECUTIVE AND THE COURTS

CHAPTER XIX

EXECUTIVE IMMUNITY FROM JUDICIAL CONTROL

THE questions which arise for consideration under this branch of the subject are not questions involving the direct assumption by one of the departments of power vested in the others, but rather questions concerning the indirect control by one of these departments of powers exercised by the others.

Notwithstanding that the logical application of the principle of the independence of the departments would require that the acts and persons of each department should be free from the interference and control of any other department, in practice there is a great conflict as to whether theory should not under particular circumstances give way to justice.

In some jurisdictions the courts, in bold defiance of theory, do not scruple to issue the writ of mandamus against the chief executive officer of the commonwealth to compel the performance of executitive duties. Although it is universally conceded that the writ will never issue to control the governor's discretionary powers, yet his ministerial duties, upon whose performance individual rights may depend, have sometimes been held amenable to the compulsory process of the courts, irrespective of the fact whether such ministerial powers were conferred by statute or the constitution.[1] If in addition to his

[1] State *vs.* Governor, 5 Ohio St. 528; Cotten *vs.* Governor, 7 Jones (N. C.) 545; *contra*, Chamberlain *vs.* Sibley, 4 Minn. 309; R. R Co. *vs.* Moore, 36 Ala. 371.

executive powers, or among his executive powers, the constitution devolves upon the governor ministerial duties, such as the issuing of commissions to persons whose election has been duly certified, a mandamus will lie against him to compel the performance of such duties.[1]

Some courts declare it difficult to understand how a duty can be any less ministerial, or can be endowed with a political nature, merely by requiring it to be performed by the governor instead of some inferior officer, or why, if it is competent for the legislature to impose upon the governor a ministerial duty, he should not be held responsible for its due execution, and be regarded *quoad hoc* not as an executive, but as a ministerial officer.[2]

These decisions are frequently based upon a dictum of Chief Justice Marshall in Marbury *vs.* Madison,[3] to the effect that it is not by the office of the person to whom the writ is directed, but by the nature of the thing to be done, that the propriety or impropriety of issuing a mandamus is to be determined. On the ground that the acts are ministerial, the courts have issued a mandamus to compel the governor to sign a patent,[4] to canvass a vote,[5] to issue a bond and mortgage,[6] and to issue a warrant upon the custodian of a fund loaned to a railroad company by legislative authority.[7]

Although the courts may compel the governor to authenticate a bill which has become law because not vetoed or returned within a specified time,[8] yet they may not compel him to sign a bill, because this is a discretionary act.[9]

What would happen if the executive should deny the juris-

[1] Magruder *vs.* Governor, 25 Md. 173.

[2] Middleton *vs.* Governor, 30 Cal. 596.

[3] 1 Cranch, 170.

[4] Middleton *vs.* Governor, 30 Cal. 596.

[5] Chumasero *vs.* Potts, 2 Mont. 242.

[6] State *vs.* Warmouth, 22 La. Ann. 1; People *vs.* Bissell, 19 Ill. 229.

[7] R. R. Co. *vs.* Moore, 36 Ala. 371.

[8] Harpending *vs.* Knight, 39 Cal. 189.

[9] Hatch *vs.* Stoneman, 66 Cal. 632.

diction of the courts to issue the mandamus against him, these cases leave unanswered. It is very doubtful whether the chief executive would be inclined to enforce against himself punishment for contempt of court, which would be the only conceivable remedy for the courts in such a case.

On the other hand, a greater weight of authority withholds from the courts the right of controlling or in any manner interfering with the powers or acts of the chief executive. The decisions to this effect stand upon a more logical if not a more just foundation. All duties imposed upon the governor, whether by statute or the constitution, they regard as executive and beyond the the control of the courts, even if the same power, if exercised by any other officer, could be controlled by the courts.[1] While he continues in the exercise of his office, the governor is answerable for his official misconduct only to the legislature through its power of impeachment. The effect of such a judicial remedy would be to deprive the people of the commonwealth of one of the departments of government.[2] The courts have no power to compel either of the other departments of government to perform its duties, any more than either of those departments can compel the courts to perform their duties. Courts have no means and no power to avoid the effects of non-action by the legislature or the executive.[3] If by a treaty, for instance, a sum of money is to be paid to a foreign nation, it becomes the duty of Congress to make the necessary appropriation, but in the nature of things this is a duty the performance of which cannot be coerced. This subject underwent much discussion at the time of the treaty of 1794, known as Jay's Treaty, at the time of the purchase of Alaska, and in the case of the award in favor of England by the Halifax Commission.

[1] Hawkins *vs.* Governor, 1 Ark. 570.

[2] Low *vs.* Towns, 8 Ga. 360; Dennet *vs.* Governor, 32 Me. 508.

[3] Myers *vs.* English, 9 Cal. 341.

That there must be an adequate remedy for every wrong, that where a clear right exists there must be a mode of enforcing that right, is true only in theory. For instance, a party may be deprived of a right by a wrong verdict, or an erroneous ruling of a judge; a person lawfully chosen to the legislature may have his seat given by the house to another, and be thus wronged without a remedy; a just claim against the government may be rejected by a board of auditors, and neither the governor nor the courts can give relief; a convicted person may conclusively demonstrate his innocence to the governor, and still be denied a pardon. The law must leave the final decision upon every controversy somewhere, and when that decision has been made it must be accepted as correct. The presumption is just as conclusive in favor of the executive as in favor of the judiciary.[1] In the formation of government, equal confidence was rightfully reposed in each department to which independent duties were assigned. If the court unintentionally errs, there is no remedy, and the same is true of the executive.[2] Accordingly, the courts have refused to issue process to compel the governor to deposit in the office of the secretary of state a bill which was not returned with objections within the specified time,[3] or to call an election to fill vacancies.[4] Nor would the courts issue a mandamus to the governor, even if he voluntarily appeared and professed a willingness to abide by the decision of the court.[5] Nor can the courts restrain the governor from issuing a certificate of election, whether he acts rightfully or wrongfully,[6] or from organizing a county on false census returns.[7]

These authorities further hold that an act is none the less

[1] Per Cooley, in People *vs.* Governor, 29 Mich. 320.

[2] People *vs.* Bissell, 19 Ill. 229.

[3] People *vs.* Yates, 40 Ill. 126.

[4] People *vs.* Cullom, 100 Ill. 472. See State *vs.* Governor, 25 N. J. L. 331.

[5] People *vs.* Governor, 29 Mich. 320. But see People *vs.* Bissell, 19 Ill. 229.

[6] Bates *vs.* Taylor, 87 Tenn. 319.

[7] See R. R. Co. *vs.* De Graff, 27 Minn. 1; Lacy *vs.* Martin. 39 Kan. 703.

executive because ministerial. As distinguished from judicial duties, all executive duties are ministerial. If the idea is that the duty of the executive becomes ministerial when no discretion is left as to the manner of its performance, and that then the courts may compel its performance, it follows that the judiciary can interfere wherever the executive duty is clear, but that in all cases of doubt and difficulty the responsibility rests upon the executive alone. The question whether an act coming within the range of duties of the chief executive is discretionary, political, or ministerial, cannot be determined judicially, but must be determined by the executive alone. If the court assumes the power to enforce the performance of ministerial duties, it opens the way to the exercise of executive power. The judge then can say what acts are ministerial, what discretionary, and what political, and in that manner review or overrule even political acts at his pleasure, and in so doing assume executive functions.[1]

For similar reasons the courts decline to issue a certiorari to review the acts of the chief executive of the commonwealth.[2] But acts of the governor are reviewable, and may, in fact, be annulled by the courts.

Although the courts cannot compel the performance of even constitutional duties by the executive, and will not restrain or in any manner interfere with any action proposed by him, yet acts performed by the executive, like acts of the legislature, may be judicially subjected to the test of the constitution, whenever they are claimed to have prejudiced private rights. Any act of the executive within the scope of his delegated authority is beyond revision by the courts; but, to determine whether he has acted within the scope of his authority, and, if not, to declare his acts void, is part of the judicial power of

[1] State *vs.* Warmouth, 24 La. Ann. 351; R. R. Co. *vs.* Lowry, 61 Miss. 102. See Throop, *Law of Public Officers*, sec. 793 *et seq.*, and High's *Extraordinary Legal Remedies*, sec 118, for the law of the different commonwealths.

[2] People *vs.* Hill, 126 N. Y. 497.

which the courts cannot be deprived, and which they must assume, however irksome the duty may be. Acts of the governor have been held illegal, on quo warranto proceedings. Such was the case where the governor appointed to office a person not properly qualified.[1] And where the governor attempted to fill an office not vacant, it was held that the person appointed by him could be ousted by quo warranto proceedings.[2] By the same process a court may examine into removals by the governor, and determine whether they were made in accordance with law.[3] Courts have also assumed by the writ of habeas corpus to inquire into the validity of a governor's action in ordering the surrender of a fugitive from justice, and have decided that his action was not in accordance with law.[4]

Where two individuals claim the right to an office and one obtains from the governor a commission, it is competent for the judiciary to go behind the commission, and to inquire into the validity of the election and to decide the rights of the contesting parties.[5]

The courts will prevent any one from usurping the functions or intruding into the office of the executive, and punish such usurpation.[6]

As regards the exemption of the President of the United States from judicial supervision, a dictum of the Supreme Court disclaims the power of the court to control the President,[7] and subsequently the same court refused to enjoin the President from carrying into effect an act of Congress which

[1] People *vs.* Pratt, 50 Hun, 454. [2] Dullam *vs.* Wilson, 53 Mich. 392.

[3] People *vs.* Berrien, 45 N. W. 78.

[4] People *vs.* Curtis, 50 N. Y. 321; 2 Moore on Extradition, 1016 *et seq.*

[5] Low *vs.* Towns, 8 Ga. 360.

[6] Att'y-Gen'l *vs.* Barstow, 4 Wis. 567. See State *vs.* Gleason, 12 Fla. 190. The courts will determine which of two bodies, each claiming to be the Senate, is the constitutional body. State *vs.* Rogers, 56 N. J. L. 480.

[7] Kendall *vs.* United States, 12 Pet. 524, 610.

was alleged to be unconstitutional, since the duties under it were discretionary, political and executive. The court declined to decide whether it had power to compel the President to perform or refrain from performing a ministerial act.[1]

President Jefferson said, if the Supreme Court had granted a mandamus in the case of Marbury *vs.* Madison, he should have regarded it as trenching on his appropriate sphere of duty. He instructed Madison not to deliver the commission, and said he was prepared as President of the United States to maintain his own construction of the Constitution with all the powers of the government, against any attempt by the judiciary to control what he regarded as the rightful powers of the executive and senate within their peculiar departments.[2]

Other officers of the United States the Supreme Court has held to be amenable to mandamus under certain circumstances. The court will not issue the writ to control a political or discretionary power conferred upon such an officer by Congress, or delegated to him by the President as his agent,[3] but it has assumed the power to grant a mandamus against the head of a department,[4] and against the commissioner of pensions,[5] to compel them to perform ministerial duties. In this respect there is no distinction between these officers and other inferior officers of the general government.

Where the principal officers of the commonwealth governments act as mere assistants or agents of the chief executive in the performance of a political or discretionary act, they are no more subject to the control of the court than the chief execu-

[1] Mississippi *vs.* Johnson, 4 Wall. 475.

[2] *Jefferson's Works*, vol. iv, pp. 75, 317, 372.

[3] United States *vs.* Black, 128 U. S. 40; United States *vs.* Windom, 137 U. S. 636; Gaines *vs.* Thompson, 7 Wall. 347.

[4] Kendall *vs.* United States, 12 Pet. 524; United States *vs.* Schurz, 102 U. S. 378. See United States *vs.* Guthrie, 17 How. 282.

[5] Butterworth *vs.* United States, 112 U. S. 50. See United States *vs.* Black, 128 U. S. 40.

tive himself. But where a ministerial act is required to be done independently of the executive, though in a certain sense they are executive officers, it would be as idle to dispute their liability to legal process as it would be to make the same claim to exemption on behalf of any other officer entrusted with similar duties of a lower grade. The writ has been sustained to compel the performance of ministerial duties against the secretary of state in Kansas, Louisiana, Missouri, Wisconsin and Illinois; against the comptroller in New York, California and Florida; against the auditor in Alabama, Arkansas, Iowa, Louisiana, Illinois, Michigan, Mississippi and Ohio; and against the state treasurer in Alabama, Kansas, Louisiana, Michigan and North Carolina.[1] The mandamus has been issued to compel the president of the senate, in the absence of the governor, to assume the governorship, on his refusal to do so.[2]

On the other hand, Minnesota, Louisiana, Illinois and Texas, on the ground that every act of any executive officer, even if ministerial, is executive, refuse to grant the writ under any circumstances against the principal officers of the government, as the secretary of state, state treasurer and state auditor [3]

The governor is not subject to the subpœna of the grand jury. He is the absolute judge of what official communications to himself or his agents may or may not be repeated; also, of what his official duties are, and how they are to be performed.[4] Neither the President of the United States, nor the governors of the commonwealths, nor cabinet officers, are bound to disclose in a judicial inquiry, papers or information

[1] Throop's *Law of Public Officers*, sec. 798.

[2] Barnard *vs.* Taggart, 29 Atl. Rep. 1027.

[3] Authorities collected in Throop's *Law of Public Officers*, sec. 798; High's *Extraordinary Legal Remedies*, sec. 124 *et seq.*

[4] Hartcraft's Appeal, 85 Pa. St. 433; Thompson *vs.* German Valley R. R. Co., 22 N. J. Eq. 111.

officially communicated to them, when, in their own judgment, the disclosure would on public grounds be inexpedient.[1]

While Burr's trial was progressing, President Jefferson was summoned by subpœna to appear and bring papers with him. He refused to do either.[2]

The courts cannot control executive discretion. Neither the legislature nor the courts can compel or enjoin the governor to convene the legislature on extraordinary occasions.[3] Nor can they control the executive in the exercise of his power to call out the militia in certain exigencies. The President is the exclusive and final judge as to whether such exigencies have arisen.[4]

[1] 1 *Greenleaf on Evidence*, sec. 251; 1 Wharton's *Law of Evidence*, sec. 600.

[2] 3 Burr's Trial, 37.

[3] Whitman *vs.* R. R. Co., 2 Harr. 514.

[4] Martin *vs.* Mott, 12 Wheat. 9. See People *vs.* Parker, 3 Neb. 409.

CHAPTER XX

THE POWER OF REMOVAL FOR CAUSE

THE power to remove for cause a commonwealth officer has been regarded in some jurisdictions as a judicial act, and therefore incapable of being vested by the legislature in any officer or body other than the courts.[1] But it is almost universally regarded as an administrative power, and thus capable of being conferred by the legislature upon the executive or upon administrative officers,[2] or upon the courts.[3] The removal of an officer for neglect of duty involves the exercise of administrative discretion. The grant of power to remove an officer for a certain cause implies authority to judge of the existence of the cause, and this power when vested exclusively in the executive's discretion cannot be controlled in its exercise by any other branch of the government. To institute a judicial inquiry into the cause for which the governor removed an officer, or into the propriety of his action, would be a direct attack upon the independence of the executive and a usurpation of power subversive of the constitution.[4]

Although the general view is that the courts cannot review

[1] See State *vs.* Pritchard, 36 N. J. L. 101; Dullam *vs.* Wilson, 53 Mich. 392. See also Page *vs.* Hardin, 8 B. Mon. 648; Honey *vs.* Graham, 39 Texas, 1.

[2] Donahue *vs.* Wells County, 100 Ill. 94; Stern *vs.* People, 102 Ill. 540; State *vs.* Hawkins, 44 Ohio St. 98.

[3] State *vs.* Prince, 45 Wis. 610; Keenan *vs.* Perry, 24 Tex. 253; *Ex parte* Wiley, 54 Ala. 226; State *vs.* Frazier, 48 Ga. 137; Donahue *vs.* County of Hill, 100 Ill. 94; Patton *vs.* Vaughan, 39 Ark. 211. See *Ex parte* Hennen, 13 Pet. 230.

[4] State *vs.* Doherty, 25 La. Ann. 119; State *vs.* Hawkins, 44 Ohio St. 98: State *vs.* Lamantia, 33 La. Ann. 446.

the governor's action if it is taken after a hearing,[1] yet the party to be removed must have his common law right to be heard, and an opportunity of defence.[2] In Illinois alone it is held that he need not have such opportunities unless the right to them is expressly secured.[3]

Where the governor has power to remove a public officer upon charges and notice thereof, his act is final, and cannot be reviewed by an information in the nature of a quo warranto against the person appointed in the place of the officer so removed.[4]

But the question whether the governor has the power in a particular case, or whether he has exercised it in a lawful manner, may become a question for the courts to decide, whenever a right in litigation depends upon such decision.[5]

It has been asserted that a grant to the governor of the power of removal for cause includes the power of temporary suspension by him, pending the trial of the officer for malfeasance or misfeasance in office.[6]

As to whether the grant of a like power to an administrative officer or body would comprise the power of suspension, the decisions conflict.[7]

[1] State *vs.* Hawkins, 44 Ohio St. 98.

[2] Dullam *vs.* Wilson, 53 Mich. 392. See Mechem, *Public Offices and Officers*, sec. 454. People *vs.* Fire Com'rs, 72 N. Y. 445.

[3] Donahue *vs.* Will Co., 100 Ill. 94.

[4] State *vs.* Hawkins, 44 Ohio St. 98.

[5] Page *vs.* Hardin, 8 B. Mon. 648.

[6] State *vs.* Peterson, 52 N. W. 655.

[7] The affirmative of the proposition has been maintained in Shannon *vs.* Portsmouth, 54 N. H. 183; Westberg *vs.* City of Kansas, 64 Mo. 493; *contra*, State *vs.* Jersey City, 25 N. J. L. 536; Gregory *vs.* Mayor, 113 N. Y. 416. For further consideration of this subject, see Goodnow's *Adm. Law*, vol. 2, p. 99; Mechem's *Public Office and Officers*, secs. 450, 457.

PART VI

QUASI POWERS

CHAPTER XXI

THE DELEGATION OF POWER

By analogy to well-known principles of the law of agency, it has become a settled rule of our constitutional law that a power conferred on one of the departments cannot be delegated by it to any other body or authority. Thus, the governor cannot pardon a convict on condition that the people ratify his act; a judge cannot put a certain construction on the law provided the people approve it; nor can the legislature avoid responsibility for the laws it passes.[1]

[1] People *vs.* Governor, 29 Mich. 320. Within the last year both political parties in Massachusetts advocated in their platforms, the adoption of the referendum and in the mean time it received in the legislature a vote almost sufficient to authorize its proposal to the people as a constitutional amendment. It was also considered by the recent constitutional conventions of New York and several other commonwealths.

If experience is to be heeded, the referendum is an unwise expedient.

The same forces that induce the people to elect legislators anxious to avoid the responsibility of enacting laws would operate to induce the people to approve the inferior laws proposed by them. Furthermore, were the legislatures to become mere proposing bodies, people would be even less interested than they are at present in the qualifications of the persons whom they elect. The proposed laws would under such circumstances probably be of such a nature as to deserve defeat. Finally, statistics show the public indifference to questions submitted to the popular vote, especially when we compare the number of votes cast by the people for constitutional amendments with the number cast for the election of officers. In innumerable cases desirable constitutional amendments have failed of adoption only because of the neglect of the people to vote.

The state having entrusted the legislature with the power of making laws, the legislature cannot delegate the trust to any other body, or even to the people themselves.[1] But a statute may be conditional, and its taking effect may be made to depend upon some subsequent event.[2] Thus the contingency upon which the operation of an act is made to depend, may be the action of the legislature of another commonwealth. A law which provides that insurance companies of other commonwealths shall pay in taxes and fines an amount equal to that imposed, by existing or even future laws of the commonwealths of their origin, upon companies of the enacting commonwealth seeking to do business there, when such amount is greater than that required for such purpose by the existing laws of such commonwealth, is not unconstitutional.[3]

The legislature often enacts that laws shall become effective or ineffective upon the determination by some other authority that such shall be the case. The question then arises as to whether the legislature really enacts the law, or the body whose determination was made a condition precedent to its taking effect. The proper answer would seem to depend upon the particular circumstances of each case. Thus, it is properly held that a legislative act which is complete, but of which the operative effect is dependent upon a contingency, will not necessarily be objectionable because it provides that some other body shall determine whether the contingency exists. Such body exercises no discretion, and takes no part in making any portion of the law under which it is acting. While the legislature cannot delegate its power to make a law, it can make a law delegating the power to determine some fact or

[1] Geebrick *vs.* State, 5 Ia. 491; Bradley *vs.* Baxter, 15 Barb. 522; Barto *vs.* Himrod, 8 N. Y. 438; Cooley's *Constitutional Limitations*, p. 137 n; Rice *vs.* Foster, 4 Harr. 479; 3 Law Encycl. 698.

[2] Brig *Aurora vs.* United States, 7 Cr. 382; Peck *vs.* Wedell, 17 Ohio St. 271.

[3] People *vs.* Fire Association of Phil., 92 N. Y. 311.

state of things upon which the operation of such law is to depend.[1]

Where the condition on which a general statute is made to depend is the will of the people as expressed at the polls, or otherwise, it would seem that such an act involves the delegation of legislative power to the people. The law would be made to depend upon the discretion and will of the people rather than upon the discretion and will of the legislature, in which body alone the state has vested the law-making power.[2]

But, however this may be, the legislature may enact laws to go into operation only upon the condition that they first be approved by a majority of the people of the *locality* to which they are to apply. The people of the locality would not in such a case enact a law, in the constitutional sense, but only an ordinance. Such an act has been said to be one of administration, not of legislation.[3] It would only be the exercise of an administrative or qualified legislative power, just as the passing of municipal ordinances by a municipal body is only the exercise of an administrative and not of a legislative

[1] Locke's Appeal, 72 Pa. St. 491; *Ex parte* Mato, 19 Texas App. 112.

[2] Barto *vs.* Himrod, 8 N. Y. 482. See Geebrick *vs.* State, 5 Ia. 491; State *vs.* Copeland, 3 R. I. 33; Cooley's *Const. Limitations*, p. 137. See 3 Law Encycl. 700, c. c.; State *vs.* Parker, 26 Vt. 357. In at least one case the Constitution of New York provides for a referendum—a delegation of legislative power to the people of the commonwealth. It provides that the commonwealth shall not contract a debt exceeding one million dollars unless it is authorized by a law for some single work or purpose, which law, before it takes effect, must be approved by a vote of the people at a general election, when no other law, bill or constitutional amendment is voted on.

In the fall of 1894 the legislature of New York submitted to the people of New York, Brooklyn and some neighboring towns to be affected thereby, the question of their consolidation under one municipal government. This proceeding differed from the referendum, since the vote of the people was not to be a condition precedent to any law, but only a test of the sentiment of the popular will, the legislature having reserved the right to effect consolidation or to refuse doing so irrespective of the decision of the people.

[3] Locke's Appeal, 72 Pa. St. 491.

power. If the legislature can delegate the power of local regulation to a body distinct from itself, such as a local board, there is no constitutional provision which prohibits its delegation to the people of the locality.

Conceding that the legislature may enact laws whose operation depends upon the will of an administrative board or of the people of a locality, can the legislature enact local regulations which should go into effect only upon the condition that they are approved by the courts? Enough has already been said to show that such a law would not provide for a delegation of legislative power to the courts. It would at most delegate only administrative power to the judicial tribunals. Whether a law delegating such power to the courts would be held constitutional or not, would therefore depend upon the question whether the courts regard themselves as authorized to exercise administrative powers. As to this question, the courts are in irreconcilable conflict. The conflict is due partly to the fact that acts such as those described are not distinguished from legislative acts in the constitutional sense, and courts not infrequently give as a reason for their refusal to exercise such power that it is legislative.[1] On the other hand, a majority of the courts consider such power to be administrative, and find no constitutional obstacle to its exercise.[2] Where a general statute prescribed the conditions under which the boundaries of a municipal corporation might be extended, and authorized the courts to determine whether the proper conditions existed and whether justice and equity required that territory should be annexed, it was held that the reference of these questions to the courts did not involve the delegation of legislative power, or of the power to create a corporation. The questions, it was said, were so far of a judicial

[1] Shumway *vs.* Bennett, 29 Mich. 451; People *vs.* Nevada, 6 Cal. 43.

[2] Cooley's *Constitutional Limitations*, p. 146, n. S.

character that they might properly be committed to the judicial department.[1]

In Massachusetts, where local option laws are considered valid, a distinction of some force has recently been indicated. It is there intimated that the legislature cannot refer even to the people of a locality the question whether women shall be entitled to vote at local elections, because such question is a political one of general and not local concern. The determination of the classes to be invested with political power is a purely legislative power under any circumstances, and is not within the powers of towns and cities.[2]

Any and all powers not strictly legislative, executive or judicial, and not vested by the constitution in any particular authority, the legislature may, irrespective of whether they are legislative, executive or judicial in their nature, either assume, or delegate to the executive or judicial department, or to any other authority, whether of its own creation or not, without violating the principle of the separation of governmental powers.

It is not a breach of the constitution for the legislature to delegate to an administrative officer or body, administrative powers legislative in their nature. The creation by it of a railroad commission with power to fix reasonable tolls for freight and passenger transportation, is not an unconstitutional delegation of legislative power.[3]

School Boards may be invested with general authority to establish for schools such rules and regulations as they shall deem wise.[4]

[1] City of Burlington *vs.* Leebrick, 43 Ia. 252; Wahoo *vs.* Dickinson, 36 N. W. 813; *contra,* Shumway *vs.* Bennett, 29 Mich. 451. For the constitutional basis of Local Option Laws in general, see Locke's Appeal, 72 Pa. St. 491.

[2] Op. of Judges, 160 Mass. 586. [3] R. R. Co. *vs.* Smith, 70 Ga. 694.

[4] Donahue *vs.* Richards, 38 Me. 376; B'd of Education *vs.* Minor, 23 Ohio St. 211; Hopkins *vs.* Rockport, 105 Mass. 475; Murphy *vs.* Board of Directors, 30 Ia. 429; Rulison *vs.* Post, 79 Ill. 567.

The legislature may delegate to local governmental organizations quasi-legislative powers. Properly speaking, such powers are administrative rather than legislative. The rule of the delegation of powers must be construed in the light of the immemorial usage of this country and England, which always recognized certain powers of local regulation.[1] The making, executing and interpreting of municipal ordinances and local rules and regulations, cannot under a constitution which has adopted the English form of local self-government, be included within the powers confided by the constitution to the three departments of government.

Congress may confer on the territorial governments a general authority to legislate on their own affairs. But it cannot delegate general legislative authority to the local government of the District of Columbia.[2] Congress must exercise exclusive legislative power over the District.[3]

Administrative powers of a legislative nature may be delegated to the courts, and to the executive department of the government. The legislature may delegate to the governor authority to make pilotage regulations.[4]

The legislature cannot assume any judicial power in the restricted constitutional sense, nor can it delegate such power to any other authority than the courts or judicial officers provided for by the constitution.

While the constitutions permit certain courts to be established by the legislature, the legislature cannot destroy or interfere with the courts established by the constitution itself. It may establish courts, but it does not invest the courts which it creates with judicial power. The constitution alone can do that, for all judicial power comes from that instrument, and is

[1] Cooley's *Const. Limitations*, p. 191.

[2] Roach *vs.* Van Riswick, 4 MacArthur, 171.

[3] *U. S. Const.*, art. ii, sec. 5.

[4] Martin *vs.* Withers, 135 Mass. 175.

vested by that instrument in courts and judges. An act providing for the appointment of commissioners by the general assembly, to assist a court in the performance of its duties, was held unconstitutional, as an attempt by the legislature to invest such officers with judicial rights and functions. If the act contemplated that the commissioners should be mere assistants of the court, occupying positions analogous to those of masters, commissioners, or masters in chancery, such assistants, it was held, must be selected by the courts. If the commissioners were not to be considered as judges, they could not be made to share judicial duties.[1] For the same reason, a statute authorizing parties by consent of the court to select a person to act as judge for the trial of a particular case, is void.[2] It has been further held that a clerk of a court cannot be authorized by an act to render judgments by default, the clerk being only a ministerial officer.[3] Nor is it within the power of the legislature to authorize an unofficial person to sit in the place of a judge who is disqualified.[4]

The legislature cannot delegate judicial power to the governor or any other commonwealth officer. It cannot, therefore, authorize the governor, or any other officer, to pass upon the validity of a government grant and to correct errors therein.[5]

But administrative powers of a judicial nature may be delegated to the executive department of government, as the power to remove officers for cause generally, or for specified causes. And, as has already appeared, administrative power of a judicial nature may be assumed by the legislature.

[1] See State *vs.* Noble, 21 N. E. Rep. 244; 39 Alb. Law J., 242, 257; Hutkuff *vs.* Demorest, 103 N. Y. 377; Schultz *vs.* McPhilters, 79 Ind. 373; Cohen *vs.* Hoff, 3 Brev. 500.

[2] Winchester *vs.* Ayres, 4 Ia. 104.

[3] Hall *vs.* Marks, 34 Ill. 358.

[4] Van Slyke *vs.* Insurance Co., 39 Wis. 390; State *vs.* Judges, 13 Cent. Rep. 324 and n.

[5] Hilliard *vs.* Conelly, 7 Ga. 172.

Administrative powers of a judicial nature may also be vested in officers not belonging to either of the departments.

A board of police commissioners is not a court, but an administrative body, often vested with disciplinary powers of punishment and removal. It may be authorized to regulate its own practice and procedure, and is not restricted by the limitations of a court at common law.[1]

The legislature may confer upon municipal bodies the power to judge of the election of their own members.[2]

The greatest confusion exists in the authorities as to the delegation of administrative powers of a judicial nature to officers or bodies not belonging to the judicial department of government, and as to the delegation of administrative powers of a legislative nature to judges and courts.

Congress has absolute power to legislate concerning aliens. It may permit them to land, or expel them upon any condition it sees fit to impose. It may make the right of an alien to land or remain in the country depend upon the decision of any officer or body.

The proceedings before a United States judge under the Chinese Exclusion Act of 1892, which authorized judges of the United States Courts finally to determine whether an alien should be sent out of the country or be permitted to remain, were in no sense judicial, but only administrative. The order of deportation thereunder was but a method of enforcing the return of an alien who had not complied with the conditions upon the performance of which the government had determined that his continued residence should depend.[3]

When recently the Secretary of the Treasury of the United States exercised a statutory power somewhat similar to the foregoing, the American people were amazed at the absolute power with which an administrative officer could be vested.

[1] People *vs.* Police Com'rs., 84 Hun, 65.

[2] Mayor *vs.* Morgan, 18 Am. Dec. 232.

[3] Fong Yue Ting *vs.* U. S., 149 U. S. 698.

The United States Circuit Court held that although the alien in question, an undercoachman, was a domestic servant, and therefore not prohibited by the Contract Labor Law from coming to and remaining in this country, yet since the act authorized "*the Secrctary of the Treasury in case he shall be satisfied*" that an immigrant had been allowed to land contrary to the prohibition of that law, to cause such immigrant within the period of one year after landing or entry, to be taken into custody and returned to the country from which he came, the question whether he should be deported must be determined exclusively and finally by the Secretary of the Treasury.[1]

The United States Supreme Court had already on a previous occasion declared that "although Congress might, if it saw fit, authorize courts to investigate and ascertain the facts upon which the alien's right to land or remain in this country was made by statute to depend, yet Congress might entrust the final determination of these facts to an executive officer, and if it does so, his order is due process of law, and no other tribunal, unless expressly authorized by law to do so, would be at liberty to re-examine the evidence on which he acted, or to controvert its sufficiency."

The power of Congress to expel, like the power to exclude aliens or any specified class of aliens from the country, may be exercised entirely through executive officers, or Congress may call in the aid of the judiciary to ascertain any contested facts on which an alien's right to remain in the country has been made by Congress to depend.[2]

As has often been reiterated, "No legislative body can delegate to another department of government or to any other authority its power to enact laws."[3]

[1] In re Howard, 63 Fed. Rep. 263. Happily the Secretary in deference to the opinion of the judge that the alien was a domestic servant, ordered his release, although he could not be compelled to do so. See, also, U. S. *vs.* Rogers, 65 Fed. Rep. 787.

[2] Nishimura Ekins *vs.* U. S., 142 U. S. 651.

[3] Locke on *Civil Government*, 142.

Besides being a breach of the trust and confidence reposed by the people in the legislature, an act delegating law-making power to the courts would conflict with the principle of the separation of powers. To the lasting honor of the judiciary of the United States it may be said that it has not only resisted the encroachment of one department upon the other, but has also as honestly and unhesitatingly declined to exercise any of the powers properly belonging to the legislature or the executive, when called upon to do so.

In their anxiety to avoid the assumption of any legislative power, courts have often refused to exercise administrative powers of a legislative nature, as if the constitution had provided that the courts should exercise no powers of a legislative nature.

Judging from the few reported cases in point, it would seem that the legislatures have not frequently been tempted to delegate their purely legislative authority to the courts. Most of the cases cited to sustain this conclusion are attempted delegations of administrative rather than legislative powers. It is, however, conclusively established that the courts cannot be clothed with strictly legislative powers. The legislature cannot transfer its power to judge of the election of its members to the courts, if the constitution vests that power in the legislature.[1] Courts cannot be empowered to decide which of two sections of a statute shall take effect and be law.[2] A statute cannot devolve upon the judicial department of government the duty to determine the highest rate of taxation which can be borne by a municipality without injury to its creditors at large. The courts cannot assume or control the legislative function of deciding what sum public interest requires or permits to be raised.[3] The legislature cannot empower the courts to super-

[1] State *vs.* Gilmore, 20 Kan. 551; Dalton *vs.* State, 43 Ohio St. 652.

[2] State *vs.* Young, 29 Minn. 474.

[3] Hardenburgh *vs.* Kidd, 10 Cal. 402; Munday *vs.* Rahway, 40 N. J. 338.

sede, revoke, or annul a statute, since to do so would be to exercise legislative power.[1] An act providing for a prospective determination by the courts of the validity of school rules prepared by commissioners, which shall be enforced on such approval, is void.[2] Likewise an act providing that salaries of the official reporters of a court shall be fixed by the judges by an order entered on the minutes of the court, has been said to impose legislative functions on the judiciary.[3]

As has already been said, in many of the cases above referred to, the power which has been delegated was administrative or qualified legislative power rather than purely legislative. Many of the cases, since they fail to distinguish between administrative and legislative acts, may fairly be considered as deciding that the legislature cannot delegate, nor the courts assume, legislative powers. As to whether the courts may constitutionally assume administrative powers as distinguished from legislative powers, the decisions are conflicting.

Some courts have refused to exercise such powers on the ground that only judicial powers are within their competency. Other courts have assumed to exercise only such administrative duties as are judicial in their nature, and still others have assumed administrative duties which are quasi-executive or even quasi-legislative.[4]

In California, Tennessee, and Illinois it has been held that the power to determine or change the boundaries of municipal corporations, not being judicial, cannot be conferred upon the courts.[5]

[1] Shephard *vs.* Wheeling, 30 West Virginia, 479.

[2] In re School Law Manual, 63 N. H. 574. [3] Smith *vs.* Strother, 68 Cal. 194.

[4] "No duties shall be imposed by law upon the Supreme Court or any of the judges thereof, except such as are judicial, nor shall any of the judges thereof exercise any power of appointment except as herein provided." *Const. of Wyoming*, art. 5, sec. 17.

[5] People *vs.* Nevada, 6 Cal. 143; State *vs.* Armstrong, 3 Sneed, 634; *Ex parte* Chadwell, 3 Bax. 98; Willett *vs.* Belleville, 11 La. 1; Galesburg *vs.* Hawkinson, 75 Ill. 152. See also Shumway *vs.* Bennett, 29 Mich. 451.

In Missouri[1] and Arkansas[2] the legislature may vest in the courts the power to determine whether the limits of a town should be extended or a town become incorporated.

Administrative powers such as the confirmation of the reports of commissioners of estimates and assessments may be imposed upon the courts, not because they are judicial in their nature, or because such mode of determining the question is required by the constitution, but merely from considerations of convenience and general propriety.[3] If the exercise of such administrative powers would be unconstitutional, the power of reviewing, controlling and amending administrative acts could not be exercised by or delegated to the courts.[4] The power of the court exercised under the clause of the constitution[5] providing that compensation for private property taken for public use "shall be ascertained by a jury, or by not less than three commissioners appointed by a court of record, as shall be prescribed by law," is administrative and not judicial, and an act is not invalid because it authorizes the taking of lands outside the territorial jurisdiction of the court appointing the commissioners.[6]

It is now generally conceded that a judge may exercise extra-judicial powers as a commissioner. The case of the United States against Todd[7] is regarded as having decided only that if the power conferred upon the court, of passing upon the validity of pension claims, was a judicial function, the act was void because it made a judicial decision reviewable by a department other than the judicial; that, if it was not a judicial function, it could not be conferred upon the court, and that the

[1] Kayser *vs.* Trustees, 16 Mo. 88.

[2] Foreman *vs.* Town of Mariana, 43 Ark. 324.

[3] Matter of Trustees of N. Y. P. E. Pub. School, 31 N. Y. 574.

[4] See Goodnow, *The Writ of Certiorari*, 6 Political Science Quarterly, 493; Goodnow, *The Executive and the Courts*, 1 P. S. Q., 533.

[5] *Constitution of New York*, art. 1, sec. 7.

[6] In re City of Buffalo, 15 N. Y. Supp. 858. [7] 13 Howard 52, note.

act *could not be construed* as authorizing the judges composing the court to exercise the power out of court in the character of commissioners. Acts of Congress empowering judges in pursuance of treaty stipulations to examine and adjudge claims for injuries sustained by applicants, are valid. Such acts do not confer any powers on the courts of which the judges are members; but the judges act as *commissioners*, and as such may be directed to report their decision with the evidence upon which it is based to the Secretary of the Treasury for his discretionary action thereon; and it is not an objection to such an act that it does not provide an appeal from the award of the judges to the Supreme Court of the United States.[1]

Certainly the judges are at liberty to decline to act as commissioners.[2] Thus we find Judges Sharswood and Hare in 1860 writing to Governor Parker refusing to become members of the Public Building Commission.[3] The Massachusetts courts say that their judges cannot as commissioners appoint supervisors of election because the constitution does not allow judges to hold any such office.[4]

Whether the quasi-executive power to appoint officers other than those whose business pertains to the courts can be vested

[1] United States *vs.* Fereira, 13 How. 40. These cases are commented upon in Int. Commerce Commission *vs.* Brimson, 154 U. S. 447. Mr. Justice Brewer has lately accepted a position on the Venezuelan Boundary Commission, which is to report the result of its investigations to the executive and legislative departments for their further consideration. A Justice of the Supreme Court of the United States ought always seriously to consider the nature of the commission of which he is asked to become a member, especially where his membership will require the performance of extrajudicial duties of a political nature. The history of the Electoral Commission of 1876, of which three justices of the Supreme Court were members, is too well known to require comment.

[2] In re Appointment of Member of Board of Review, 27 Weekly Law Bull. 334.

[3] 8 Am. Law Reg. See also "Extra-Judicial Duties of Judges," Legal Int., vol. 35, p. 16.

[4] Case of Supervisors of Election, 114 Mass. 247; *contra*, State *vs.* George, 29 Pac. Rep. 356; In re Cincinnati Citizens, 2 Flipp. 228. Administrative officers may be removed by the courts. In re Eaves, 30 Fed. Rep. 21.

in the courts by statute, has also been questioned in some jurisdictions. The power to appoint election commissioners not having been characterized by the constitution as a legislative, executive, or judicial power, that instrument does not prohibit the legislature from authorizing the county courts to appoint such commissioners,[1] commissioners of public parks, and similar officers.[2] The circuit courts of the United States appoint supervisors of election.[3] But the courts of Massachusetts and Michigan hold that they cannot be authorized to exercise such quasi-executive powers, so as to appoint supervisors of election[4] and surveyors.[5]

The *legislative power* to incorporate a locality includes the power to fix its boundary, notwithstanding that private rights may thereby be affected.[6] The legislature may delegate to local bodies or boards of officers the power to determine the extent of territory to be included within the corporate limits, and what property and what persons shall accordingly be subject to municipal rule and taxation.[7] Though the execution of this power involves the exercise of discretion and ot power legislative in its nature, in most jurisdictions the courts have entertained no difficulty in executing it.[8]

An act allowing judges to hold special terms at discretion, and authorizing them to designate the time for holding district

[1] People *vs.* Hoffman, 116 Ill. 587.

[2] People *vs.* Morgan, 90 Ill. 558; People *vs.* Williams, 51 Ill. 63.

[3] 1 U. S. St. at Large, sec. 2012; *Ex parte* Siebold, 100 U. S. 371; In re Cincinnati Citizens, 2 Flipp. 228; Russell *vs.* Cooly, 69 Ga. 215.

[4] Supervisors of Election, 114 Mass. 247.

[5] Houseman *vs.* Montgomery, 58 Mich. 364.

[6] Galesburg *vs.* Hawkinson, 75 Ill. 153; Kelly *vs.* Pittsburgh, 104 U. S. 78.

[7] People *vs.* Carpenter, 24 N. Y. 86.

[8] State *vs.* Armstrong, 3 Sneed, 634; Keyser *vs.* Trustees, 16 Mo. 88; *Ex parte* Cadwell, 3 Bax. 98; City of Wahoo *vs.* Dickinson, 36 N. W. 318; Willet *vs.* Belleville, 11 Ga. 1. Comp. Shumway *vs.* Bennett, 29 Mich. 451; People *vs.* Nevada, 6 Cal. 143.

courts in newly organized counties within their districts, does not involve a delegation of legislative powers.[1]

It has been held that the legislature may delegate to the courts the quasi-legislative function of determining whether a proposed local improvement shall be undertaken.[2]

An act authorizing courts on application to order the building of a bridge over a stream forming a boundary between two towns,[3] or on the application of local authorities, and upon notice, to require railroad corporations to erect and maintain gates at crossings with attendants to open and close them, is not an unconstitutional grant of legislative powers to the courts.[4]

In naturalizing aliens, courts exercise an administrative power delegated to them not by a commonwealth but by the United States government. Congress adopted the commonwealth tribunals as its agents to exercise this power. The concurrence of the commonwealth legislation adds the sanction of the commonwealth to this delegation of power to the courts. That the act of the court in exercising the power is lawful, is not questioned.[5] The commonwealth legislatures may forbid the commonwealth courts to naturalize aliens, or may regulate their exercise of the power.[6]

An evidently non-judicial administrative power exercised by judges and not questioned, is their power to solemnize marriages.[7]

The legislative delegation to the courts of the power to allow or to disallow coroner's bills of fees and expenses incident to

[1] Grinad *vs.* State, 34 Ga. 270; *Ex parte* Mato, 19 Tex. App. 112.

[2] Bryant *vs.* Robins, 70 Wis. 258.

[3] Matter of Towns of Mt. Morris and Castile, 41 Hun. 29.

[4] People *vs.* L. I. R. R. Co., 47 St. R. 648.

[5] State *vs.* Penney, 10 Ark. 621.

[6] State *vs.* Judges, 32 Atl. Rep. 743.

[7] See *N. Y. Laws*, 1889, chap. 415.

inquests, was upheld, where such power had been exercised under a statute for thirty-five years.[1]

Doubts have arisen as to whether acts like those above described, when performed by the courts, are reviewable. It has been said: "Duties of this class, and they are very numerous, necessarily take their character from the departments to which they are respectively assigned. The same power which when exercised by one class of officers not connected with the judiciary would be regarded and treated as purely administrative, becomes at once judicial when exercised by a court of justice. And since judicial power in the constitutional sense is the power pertaining to courts of justice (Webster's definition), or power belonging to or emanating from a judge as such, or the authority vested in judges (Bouvier's definition), it has been held that such administrative powers when exercised by a court become judicial and reviewable by a higher court," if at all.

When similar powers are vested in the officers of the executive department, they upon a like principle ought to be regarded as executive. But where such powers are conferred upon administrative officers not belonging to either of the three departments of government, the legislature may authorize the courts to review, supervise, control, and even amend or modify their acts, whether legislative, executive, or judicial in character, because in such a case the courts would at most be called upon to exercise only administrative powers.

The Interstate Commerce Comission is not an "inferior court" of the United States. It is an administrative, not a judicial, body, and exercises administrative, not judicial, powers. Its members do not possess the constitutional tenure of office during good behavior. Congress may make its findings *prima facie* evidence in judicial proceedings.[2]

[1] Locke *vs.* Speed, 62 Mich. 408.

[2] Kentucky Bridge Co. *vs.* R. R. Co. 37 Fed. Rep. 567. See Int. Com. Commission *vs.* Brimson, 154 U. S. 447.

CHAPTER XXII

ADMINISTRATIVE OFFICES AND OFFICERS

GREAT misconception has pervaded the authorities as to the content of the departments established by the constitution, especially the executive department.

Considering the purpose for which the distributing clause was inserted in the constitutions, it becomes evident that the clause means that the powers of the *central* government—not of the *local* governments—shall be divided into three departments, and that the members of one department shall have no part or lot in the management of the affairs of either of the other central departments. The departments of which the constitutions speak and in respect to which they provide that no person employed in one shall be employed in either of the other two, are the *departments of the central government, as expressly defined and limited in the constitutions*, and mean that no member of the *legislative department, as defined in the constitutions*, shall at the same time be a member of the *executive or judicial department as therein defined;* and vice versa. The constitution only forbids persons charged with the exercise of powers belonging to one department from exercising functions pertaining to the others. But the powers thus referred to must be powers which in their essential nature strictly belong to one of the other departments as defined in the constitution, or which are in express terms conferred upon one of the other departments.[1]

Powers of local government, whether legislative, executive, or judicial in their nature, may each and all be exercised by the

[1] People *vs.* Provines, 34 Cal. 520.

same body, or may each and all be exercised by one of the three constitutional departments, as far as the distributing clauses are concerned. Quasi-legislative, quasi-judicial, or quasi-executive powers may be conferred upon the courts, or reviewed and modified by the courts, without violating the principle of the separation of powers.[1]

The question has been raised, whether, in spite of the distributing clause and of the constitutional provision that the judicial powers of the commonwealth shall be vested in a supreme court, and in such inferior courts as the legislature may from time to time order and establish, and in justices of the peace, the legislature can confer the judicial powers of justices of the peace on the mayors of municipalities.

In Louisiana, under a constitutional provision like that just stated, such an act was held valid,[2] but under a constitutional provision that the judicial power should be vested in a supreme court, district courts, and in justices of the peace, such act was held unconstitutional.[3]

In Maryland an act of incorporation provided that the mayor should have all the powers of justices of the peace. Subsequently a revised constitution was adopted vesting all judicial powers of the commonwealth in certain enumerated courts and in the justices of the peace. It was held that the new constitution stripped the mayor of all judicial power or jurisdiction appertaining to the office of justice of the peace, but did not deprive him of the police powers of justices of the peace as conservator of the peace.[4]

[1] Where an appeal from the assessment of a corporation by a proper officer was authorized to be taken to a court, it was held that the conclusion by the court upon the appeal was in no proper sense a judgment, but only an assessment, and therefore error would not lie upon it. Auditor Gen'l *vs.* Pullman Co., 34 Mich. 59. See *Writ of Certiorari*, 6 Pol. Sc. Q. 493; *The Executive and the Courts*, 1 Pol. Sc. Q. 533.

[2] Baton Rouge *vs.* Dearing, 15 La. Ann. 208.

[3] Lafon *vs.* Dufrocq, 9 La. Ann. 350.

[4] Hagerstown *vs.* Dechert, 32 Md. 369.

In Illinois, North Carolina, and Maryland it is held that the mayor cannot be invested with the judicial powers of justices of the peace;[1] that the mayor of the city has no judicial power under the constitution, and that therefore the legislature can confer none upon him.[2]

But the better and more prevalent opinion seems to be that the distributing and judiciary clauses of the constitutions were not intended to deprive the mayor of the judicial powers which he has always exercised. In a majority of the jurisdictions it is held that the legislature can confer the judicial powers of justices of the peace upon the mayor.[3] In New Jersey it has been held that the powers of the justices of the peace may be conferred upon the mayor, recorder, and aldermen of a city or borough.[4]

The objection to the same person holding the office of mayor and justice of the peace (under the criminal laws of the commonwealth) is that the mayor is an executive officer, and that judicial authority is conferred upon him in conflict with that provision of the constitution which says no person charged with the exercise of powers properly belonging to one of the departments—the executive, the legislative, or the judicial—shall ever exercise any functions appertaining to either of the others. These departments are the departments of the government of the commonwealth. The mayor of the city is not a part of the government of the commonwealth. He exercises none of the functions belonging to that department. Whatever executive offices he may perform pertain to him only as an officer of the corporation. He is not an executive officer in any proper sense.[5]

[1] State *vs.* Maynard, 14 Ill. 419; Beesman *vs.* Peoria, 16 Ill. 484; Hagerstown *vs.* Dechert, 32 Md. 369.

[2] Town of Edenton *vs.* Wool, 65 N. C. 379.

[3] Robinson *vs.* Benton County, 49 Ark. 49; Bain *vs.* Mitchell, 82 Ala. 304; State *vs.* Ziegler, 32 N. J. L. 262; Gulick *vs.* New, 14 Ind. 93.

[4] Hutchings *vs.* Scott, 4 Halst. 218.

[5] Santo *vs.* State, 2 Iowa, 165.

The executive and administrative duties of the mayor are not within the executive and administrative departments established by the constitution. In respect to such duties the mayor is merely an officer of the municipal corporation, and he may discharge the duties of justice of the peace and his corporate functions at the same time without violating the constitution. The judicial duties of the mayor are not incidental to his municipal office, for he is clothed in this respect with a general power to administer judicially the laws of the commonwealth. The mayor acting both as mayor and judge, sits in two capacities. Thus the same act may on the same day be punished by him once as mayor acting for the city, and once as a judge, for violation of the laws of the commonwealth. Though he would act in two capacities or offices, only one of them would be an office under the commonwealth.[1]

On the ground that the distributing clause means that the powers of the commonwealth government—not local governments—are divided into three departments, and the members of one department shall have no part or lot in the management of the affairs of either of the other departments, the police judge of a city and county may hold and perform the duties of the office of police commissioner of the same city and county as an *ex officio* officer thereof.[2] In Arkansas no person can at the same time hold the office of treasurer of the state and justice of the peace. The office of state treasurer, as well as the offices of secretary of state, auditor, treasurer, attorney general, sheriff, deputy-sheriff, coroner, constable, and military offices, are executive, and belong to the executive department; for the constitution of the commonwealth assigns them to that division of power and makes all their duties necessarily of an executive character, whereas the office of justice of the peace is as much a judicial office as the office of a supreme judge.[3]

[1] Waldo *vs.* Wallace, 12 Ind. 569.

[2] People *vs.* Provines, 34 Cal. 520.

[3] State *vs.* Hutt, 2 Ark. 282; Banks *vs.* Curran, 10 Ark. 142. See Oliver *vs.* Martin, 36 Ark. 137.

Although the recorder of the city of Philadelphia possessed some powers and performs some duties of a judicial nature, he was not a judge within the terms, spirit, and meaning of the constitutional provision that no officer under the United States should be a judge in Pennsylvania.[1]

The question has also arisen as to whether officers like the mayor, when exercising the powers of justices of the peace, are included in the constitutional provisions which relate to the eligibility of judicial officers to other than judicial office. A mayor exercising such powers has been held to be a judicial officer, and therefore ineligible to the office of sheriff under a a constitutional provision which declares: "No person elected to any judicial office shall during the term be eligible to any office of trust or profit under the state other than a judicial office."[2] He is also in the same commonwealth ineligible to the office of prison director during the time in which he is mayor.[3]

Though the constitution expressly declare that the judicial power of the commonwealth shall be vested in a supreme court, district courts, and justices of the peace, the legislature may establish local tribunals, usually called municipal courts, and authorize them to punish violations of municipal ordinances. The power of punishing violations of municipal ordinances is an administrative, or at most a qualified judicial, power, and not a judicial power in the strict sense of that term. An act in violation of municipal police regulations is an offence against the municipality and not against the laws of the commonwealth, and is therefore not a crime.

Power to create municipal corporations necessarily includes the power to authorize them to make by-laws and ordinances for the government of the inhabitants, and also the

[1] Commonwealth *vs.* Dallas, 4 Dallas, 229.

[2] Gulick *vs.* New, 14 Ind. 93; Waldo *vs.* Wallace, 12 Ind. 569.

[3] Howard *vs.* Shoemaker, 35 Ind. 111.

power to authorize them to enforce such ordinances. The ability to enforce ordinances is just as essential to the good government of the municipality as the power to enact them. "The administration of judicial ordinances is the exercise of a sort of judicial power, but no part of the judicial power contemplated by the section of the constitution referred to. *That section refers to the enforcement of the laws of the commonwealth at large.* The constitutional courts there named have exclusive cognizance of all subjects arising directly under the laws of the legislature or at common law or in chancery, but it was not intended that in them alone could power to enforce city ordinances be deposited."[1] It would be impossible for a large city to preserve order if in every case it were a necessary preliminary that the offender should be regularly prosecuted, indicted, and tried. Under the police power of the municipality, a person disturbing the public peace, a person guilty of a nuisance or of obstructing the highways, or guilty of like offences, may be summarily arrested, fined, or even imprisoned, without infringing the judicial power of the constitution. Thus, where a mayor was authorized by a municipal ordinance to try and fine disorderly persons found within the corporate limits, it was held that the power was not in the sense of the constitution a part of the judicial power. It was part of the police power, as contradistinguished from the regular judiciary powers of the commonwealth.[2] But a contrary view was entertained in Louisiana, where it was held that for the violation of an ordinance the corporation should resort to the judicial tribunals organized under the constitution, and that an act conferring power in such case on the mayor was void.[3]

Since local officers are neither legislative, executive, nor judicial within the restrictions of the distributing clause, the legislature may vest in them either purely executive or judi-

[1] State *vs.* Young, 3 Kansas, 445. [2] Shafer *vs.* Mumma, 17 Md. 331.

[3] Lafon *vs.* Dufrocq, 9 La. Ann. 350.

cial powers of the commonwealth without violating that clause. Therefore the legislature may, if there is no express constitutional restriction, vest in local tribunals or officers, like the mayor, jurisdiction over cases arising *under the laws of the commonwealth*, that is, even vest in them jurisdiction over crimes. In such case the legislature makes use of the local officers or institutions as direct agencies of the commonwealth.[1] When such tribunals are by constitutional or statutory provisions vested with such limited civil or criminal jurisdiction over offences against the commonwealth laws, their actions in regard to such jurisdiction become judicial in the most limited sense of that term, and are not merely administrative. Therefore prosecutions in such courts for violations of the criminal laws of the commonwealth should be carried on in the name of the government, but there is no propriety in requiring that the commonwealth should be a party to every petty prosecution under the police regulations of a municipal corporation.[2] The question whether a municipal court is acting as an administrative or judicial tribunal may become of great importance. Where the legislature or the municipality itself undertakes to confer on municipal courts summary jurisdiction of criminal offences, and the constitution provides that no freeman shall be put to answer a criminal charge but by indictment, nor be convicted of any crime but by the verdict of a jury of good and lawful men, such acts are void.[3] Where a constitution requires presentment and indictment, and a statute dispenses with the necessity of these, the statute is void, and the trial in a city court under such statute is *coram non judice* and cannot form a bar to a subsequent indictment for the same cause.[4] There can be no summary conviction under an ordi-

[1] *Ex parte* Slattery, 3 Ark. 485; Rector *vs.* State, 6 Ark. 187.

[2] Davenport *vs.* Bird, 34 Iowa, 524.

[3] State *vs.* Moss, 2 Jones (N. C.) 66.

[4] Rector *vs.* State, 6 Ark. 187.

nance for that which is a criminal offence by the general laws of the commonwealth.[1]

The provision of the United States Constitution, that "trials of all crimes except in cases of impeachment shall be by jury," is to be construed in the light of the principles which at common law determined whether or not a person accused of a crime was entitled to be tried by a jury. But the violation of municipal ordinances concerning local affairs in respect to matters non-criminal in their nature, may be proceeded against in a summary manner.[2] Offences against ordinances proper made in virtue of the implied or incidental powers of corporations, or in the exercise of their legitimate police authority for the preservation of the peace, good order, safety, and health, and which relate to minor acts and matters not embraced in the public criminal statutes of the commonwealth, are not usually or properly regarded as criminal,[3] and hence need not necessarily be prosecuted by indictment or tried by a jury.[4]

In view of the recent reform movements in municipal government, it may be said that although a concentration of the powers of municipal government in the same hands is not a violation of the principle of the separation of governmental powers, it may be a violation of common sense. Much might be gained, if the powers of local self-government bestowed upon municipalities were distributed among the principal municipal departments, in a manner similar to that in which powers are distributed in the central government.[5]

[1] People *vs.* Slaughter, 2 Douglass (Mich.) 334.

[2] Callan *vs.* Wilson, 127 U. S. 540.

[3] *Ex parte* Hollwedell, 74 Mo. 395.

[4] Williamson *vs.* Augusta, 4 Ga. 509; Byers *vs.* Commonwealth, 42 Pa. St. 89, 94. See Dillon on Municip. Corp., Sec. 427 et. seq.

[5] See "An American View of Municipal Government in the United States," by Seth Low. Bryce's Am. Com., chap. 52.

NOTE.—On p. 140, *supra*, the case of People *vs.* Angle, 109 N. Y., 564, is cited, to the effect that the civil service law of New York could not apply to the Department of Public Works for the reason that, by the Constitution then in force, the power of appointment vested in the head of that department was exclusive, and not subject to restriction by act of the legislature. In the case of People *vs*, Roberts, decided by the Court of Appeals February 18, 1896, 148 N. Y., 360, it has been held that under the new Constitution of New York, which went into effect January 1, 1895, appointments by the Superintendent of Public Works are subject to the civil service law. The case of People *vs.* Angle is, therefore, no longer law.